THE
POWER
TO
CHANGE

Mastering the Habits That Matter Most

WORKBOOK | 15 LESSONS

CRAIG GROESCHEL

Harper*Christian*
Resources

The Power to Change Workbook
© 2023 by Craig Groeschel

Requests for information should be addressed to:
HarperChristian Resources, 3900 Sparks Dr. SE, Grand Rapids, Michigan 49546

ISBN 978-0-310-15081-7 (softcover)
ISBN 978-0-310-15082-4 (ebook)

Craig Groeschel is represented by Thomas J. Winters of Winters & King, Inc., Tulsa, Oklahoma.

First Printing February 2023 / Printed in the United States of America

CONTENTS

INTRODUCTION

Change may be the only constant in life, but experiencing the changes you want to see in your life often remains elusive. Few struggles are more frustrating and pervasive than knowing you want to change but, despite wanting and trying to change, finding it won't stick. Perhaps you've tried to eliminate certain habits and behaviors in the past and made progress for a while, only to revert to your default patterns. You know all too well how it feels on the proverbial one-step-forward-two-steps-back treadmill.

Maybe you want to take better care of your body by eating healthy food and exercising regularly. But that means giving up comfort foods like chips and ice cream and finding time to work out in your already hectic schedule. You might want to give up smoking once and for all, and have tried everything, only to light up again when stress ramps up at work. It could be your spending habits and how you handle money. It might be that you want to change the sites and images you visit online. Or you see certain patterns in the ways you parent that you wish you could change. Or you would like to pray and spend time in God's Word on a consistent daily basis.

Nearly everyone has certain bad habits that they want to eliminate and other healthy ones they wish they could practice regularly. But no matter how hard you try to give up some things, they always seem to boomerang back into your life. And no matter how many times you begin healthier habits, they eventually fall by the wayside.

You want to change.

But so far it hasn't worked.

You want your life to be different.

You want to be different.

But you're so tired. Exhausted, even. Shame hovers around your past failed attempts. Obstacles and barriers seem to pop up whenever you try. You want to see growth and healing physically, mentally, emotionally, and spiritually. But you feel desperate and powerless to change based on what you've tried so far. You may even hate yourself for not being stronger or having more willpower, for always seeming to give in rather than hang on and resist.

Regardless of what you want to stop doing and start doing, you know you're stuck. You've wanted that big "something" (and a few other things, too) to change for years, but you can't seem to crack the code. You've given up on finding a silver bullet and resigned yourself to settling for less than your heart longs to experience. You may feel angry and even cynical about your ability to change at this point in your life.

So you're probably wondering why this time should be any different. Why you should expect reading *The Power to Change* and using this workbook to help you experience lasting change when so many past programs, goals, resolutions, books, workbooks, seminars, retreats, and conferences haven't produced the results you crave.

Simply put, it's time to change the way you think about change.

It's time to rely on a greater power source than your will and determination.

Because you *can* change.

God has promised that change is possible for you.

Change eluded you in prior attempts because your methods and motives were temporary, ineffective, and disconnected from the right power source. But the good news is that you can learn how to change. It's never too late to reevaluate the way you think about yourself, God, and the habits you want to make and break.

As you read *The Power to Change*, this workbook will help you go deeper and implement the important truths essential to changing your mindset and behavior. Following the key principles in the book, you will adopt strategies to address what is going on below the surface of your desire to change. You will gain a greater understanding of what is required for lasting changes in your life.

Equipped with new insight and empowered by your faith in God, you will discover a path forward free of past baggage and present obstacles. You can learn to access the power to change by mastering the habits that matter most. If you're tired of settling for less, tired of being tired, and tired of gimmicks that never work, then you're in a good place to experience ongoing power for lasting change. If you're ready to start living the life you've been hoping for and dreaming about, then let's get started.

It's time, once and for all, to discover the power to change!

PART 1

WHO. NOT DO.

Lasting change results from discovering the truth about who you are and not from simply tweaking what you do. In order to understand that change requires more than modifying your behavior, you must reconsider how you think of yourself, your relationship with God, and your future self. This process requires you to examine how and why you view yourself—and God—the way you do. As you begin identifying false assumptions about who you are and replacing them with who God says you are, you take a giant step toward lasting change. Here are the key principles you will learn in part 1:

- To experience change that lasts, focus on *who*, not *do*.
- You do what you do because of what you think of you.
- To change what you *do*, you need to first change what you *think* of you.
- You are who God says you are.
- You *will* change, and you *can* become who you want to become.
- If your do is about who God wants you to become, about who you want to become, then your do is not small.
- To change, you need to think the right thing about yourself, know your true identity, and start your identity with who, not do.

WHY YOU DO WHAT YOU DO

Who we are shapes our character and our thoughts about ourselves and others. What we think within ourselves, we are.

CRAIG GROESCHEL

If someone had been writing about the same topics, themes, and issues for more than ten years, you would probably consider them an expert. If this person sent out a weekly newsletter to more than two million subscribers, you might assume they're well respected. If this well-respected expert wrote a #1 *New York Times* bestseller that has sold more than nine million copies and been translated into more than fifty languages, you would conclude that he is a phenomenal writer.[1]

James Clear, best known for his contemporary classic book *Atomic Habits*, fits all of these descriptions. Yet he didn't just wake up one day and decide to be an expert on habits, decision-making, and continuous improvement before writing a mega-bestselling book that continues to change lives worldwide. He started by examining why he struggled to change certain behaviors and writing about his findings. And he began implementing his findings to form habits that reflected who he was becoming.

Clear admits, "For most of my early life, I didn't consider myself a writer. If you were to ask any of my high school teachers or college professors, they would tell you I was an average writer at best: certainly not a standout. When I began my writing career, I published a new article every Monday and Thursday for the first few years. As the evidence grew, so did my identity as a writer. I didn't start out as a writer. I became one through my habits."[2]

- How does James Clear's example resonate with you? In what ways can you relate to his process of becoming a writer?

- Just as James Clear became a writer through the habit of writing, how has an aspect of your identity been shaped by your practice of a certain habit?

- What is the relationship between the habits you want to change and the way you see yourself? How have you usually thought about your identity in past attempts to change certain habits?

- If you were able to eliminate your worst habit and replace it with a healthy one, how would you see yourself differently?

EXPLORING GOD'S WORD

The Bible is clear that wanting to change and trying harder aren't enough. Based on past attempts, you know your motivation and willpower are limited resources that circumstances, relationships, and moods can quickly deplete. No matter how often or how differently you modify your behavior, they don't equip you with the power to sustain the changes you desire. The main reason you haven't experienced lasting change stems from putting your attention, energy, and focus on what you do rather than what you think about yourself.

God's Word reveals that you have to shift your focus to changing your thoughts rather than trying to change your actions. The wisdom of Proverbs explains, "For as he thinks within himself, so he is" (23:7 NASB). In other words, the thoughts running through your mind shape your perspective and attitude about who you think you are. Based on your life events, interactions with others, and most importantly, your responses—especially internally—you form a story that you tell yourself.

While your mindset and self-narrative is unique and personally complex, it will often tilt toward one end of the spectrum or the other. On one extreme, you view yourself as a victim of your circumstances and the choices of others. You feel powerless to make changes and give up trying. You basically believe that change is impossible.

The other extreme is being an overcomer: accepting events that can't be changed and taking responsibility for your response. You make choices based on what is true and follow through with actions. You trust God to transform your thinking and empower your decisions. This is the approach Paul advocates in Romans 12:

¹ And so, dear brothers and sisters, I plead with you to give your bodies to God because of all he has done for you. Let them be a living and holy sacrifice—the kind he will find acceptable. This is truly the way to worship him. ² Don't copy the behavior and customs of this world, but let God transform you into a new person by changing the way you think. Then you will learn to know God's will for you, which is good and pleasing and perfect.

ROMANS 12:1-2 NLT

- What word or phrase jumps out at you in this passage? Why is it significant?

- What does it mean for you to "let God transform you into a new person by changing the way you think"?

- How does this passage from Romans reinforce Proverbs 23:7 (see above)?

- Based on your experience, do you agree that your thoughts—not your behaviors—are the key to lasting change? Why or why not?

EMBRACING THE TRUTH

God's Word says that your identity directly determines the decisions you make. As you've seen, Romans and Proverbs reveal this truth explicitly, and you'll find more examples from Scripture in lessons to come. Whether you're aware of it or not, you do what you do because of what and how you think about yourself.

Your identity may seem like an undetected current below the surface of your life. Other times, you may be aware of your beliefs about yourself and see that identity's riptide on your decisions and behaviors. If you think you don't deserve to be treated respectfully by your coworkers, then you won't object to their harassment. If you think you're not athletic enough to exercise regularly, then you have a default excuse for skipping workouts.

Your mental attitude explains why trying to change what you do never lasts. Your behavior doesn't exist in a vacuum. Problems come up, delays happen, and schedules crash. Your expectations about how your day will proceed don't usually include curveballs—but they come nonetheless. No matter how determined you are to behave differently, it's tough when you hit turbulence.

Studies by psychologists and social scientists continue to reinforce the biblical secret to lasting change: transform what you think of yourself, and your actions will follow. If you try to change your behavior without changing your identity, you're pulling up a weed without getting to the root. It's time to identify the mental weeds you've been allowing to grow or pulling without addressing their roots. It's time to yank out your inaccurate assumptions and false beliefs about who you are and make room for the truth of who God says you are.

- How do you internally criticize yourself most often? What conclusion have you formed based on this recurring criticism?

- Review your responses to exercise 2 at the end of chapter 1.1 in *The Power to Change*. What self-perception has had the most power to sabotage your past attempts to change? Why?

- Drawing on your answers to exercise 3 at the end of chapter 1.2 in the book, do you see any patterns or causal relationships between past attempts to change and your underlying thoughts about yourself? How are they related?

- If you're honest with yourself, which way does your mind tilt more frequently—toward viewing yourself as a victim or an overcomer? Explain your response.

CHANGING THE WAY YOU CHANGE

Many people underestimate the ways their perceptions color their self-identities in relation to their attempts to change. For example, an incident from childhood or a hurtful comment made a decade ago becomes the catalyst for someone consistently thinking of themselves as overweight no matter how much they weigh or how much weight they lose. They no longer see themselves objectively because they're subjectively locked in on past history as if it were eternal truth, which it's not. They struggle to eat healthy and exercise regularly because they falsely believe that no matter what they do, they will always be an overweight person.

When you're locked in on seeing and thinking certain ways, you lose sight of who you really are. Before you can embrace the truth of who God says you are (coming up in the next lesson), you can make the process easier by identifying your false identity-beliefs and the ways they have undermined your previous plans to change. Think of it as clearing out the old, false self-beliefs in order to make room for what is true.

Exercises 1, 2, and 3 in *The Power to Change* are a helpful start for growing in self-awareness. But if you want to go deeper, it's important to understand how your toxic self-thoughts were planted, how they've been reinforced and taken root, and how they've bloomed into false beliefs about your identity. With this as your goal, it's time to do some thought-weeding!

- What toxic thoughts repeatedly poison the way you see yourself? List at least three below and the basis or origin for each one. Here is an example to get you started:

TOXIC THOUGHT: *What needs weeding?*
I'm not smart enough.

Basis/origin: *How was it planted?*
My high school teacher told me I would never succeed.

Basis/reinforcement: *How did it take root?*
I quit college before finishing my degree.

Poison fruit: *How does it poison my identity?*
I'm not smart enough to make a plan to change and stick with it.

Now it's your turn. Be as specific as you can.

TOXIC THOUGHT #1: *What needs weeding?*

Basis/origin: *How was it planted?*

Basis/reinforcement: *How did it take root?*

Poison fruit: *How does it poison my identity?*

TOXIC THOUGHT #2: *What needs weeding?*

Basis/origin: *How was it planted?*

Basis/reinforcement: *How did it take root?*

Poison fruit: *How does it poison my identity?*

TOXIC THOUGHT #3: *What needs weeding?*

Basis/origin: *How was it planted?*

Basis/reinforcement: *How did it take root?*

Poison fruit: *How does it poison my identity?*

KEEPING THE CHANGE

The power to change begins with identifying the recurring negative thoughts about yourself that are holding you back. All too often, we don't hit pause on old thoughts but allow them to play without questioning their accuracy or validity. But now that you've started this process, you can train yourself to monitor your thoughts and "demolish arguments and every pretension that sets itself up against the knowledge of God" and "take captive every thought to make it obedient to Christ" (2 Corinthians 10:5).

Instead of allowing false beliefs and overly critical labels to rush through your mind like a runaway train, you can hit the brakes and halt the destruction they're doing to your identity. With regular practice, you will become more aware of damaging thoughts and the impact they have on the way you see yourself as opposed to your true identity in Christ. As you learn to recognize them, you can prevent them from leaving the station and gaining speed.

A great way to begin identifying and capturing these thoughts is keeping a thought journal for an entire day. To begin, just jot down any thoughts that negatively impact the way you see yourself. You can use a notepad, phone notes, this workbook, or whatever makes it easy for you to do. There's no right or wrong way to do it as long as you're able to record thoughts that prevent you from seeing yourself the way God sees you.

Start in the morning when you wake up and check in with yourself. Go beyond how you're feeling and any expectations for that day. Instead notice what you're telling yourself about yourself. Record the time and any details related to your false thinking. For instance, you might note, "Tuesday, 8:45 am, just spilled coffee on my shirt while getting in my car. Thought: *I'm so clumsy—I never do anything right!*" Or "Friday, 10:22 am, in breakroom after team meeting. Thought: *My coworkers think I'm overweight, so I might as well have another donut.*"

For now, your job is simply to record these thoughts and note the time and circumstances around them. It's important to write them down for three reasons. First, the act of writing will help you process the impact they're having on your mindset. Next, it allows you to gauge their frequency. Finally, a written record is important because you will come back to your thought journal for later exercises.

Keeping your thought journal can be painful. You may not realize just how often these comments and self-condemnations zip through your mind—which is why it's important to pray each day, if possible, every time you write down a toxic thought. Simply ask God to give you wisdom and guidance as you begin this challenging process of changing the way you think about change. Thank him for the power you have through Christ.

WHO YOU THINK YOU ARE

You will change, and you can become who you want to become.

CRAIG GROESCHEL

Impoverished kid. Abuse victim. High-school dropout. Career failure. Rejected artist. Homeless person.

Any single one of these labels has the power to limit your perception of yourself and cause you to settle for far less than the best God has for you. Any of these labels could potentially blindfold you to the truth about who you are. Any one of these can be repeated by those around you until you repeat it to yourself. Cumulatively, these challenges produce a barrier that might leave you feeling desperate, hopeless, resigned to defeat.

Yet these descriptors only have power to define you if you let them. These are only a few of the labels Tyler Perry faced throughout his early life. "My childhood was a story of discouragement, belittlement, and unthinkable abuse, and yet I rose above," he writes in his inspirational memoir *Higher Is Waiting*.[3] If he had accepted the names he was called, the socioeconomic limitations of his circumstances, or the residual emotional trauma of repeated sexual and physical abuse, Perry would not have become the multi-hyphenate entertainer and entrepreneur he is today.

Well known to millions worldwide for his series of movies featuring his character Madea, Tyler Perry has transcended the role to become one of the most influential people in the entertainment industry. He has written, produced, starred in, and secured the rights to more than twenty-two feature films, 1,200 television episodes, and a couple dozen stage plays.[4] He has built a 330-acre soundstage/studio outside Atlanta on land that once housed a Confederate army base during the American Civil War.[5]

These facts merely scratch the surface of this multifaceted man whose financial success adds another label to his lifelong list: billionaire. Tyler Perry has always refused to be limited by labels—and so should you.

• What labels and limiting assumptions from your childhood continue to plague your thinking? Which one troubles you most? Explain your response.

• What is one conclusion about you that others—family, friends, coworkers—have reinforced that is not necessarily true?

- What is one of your completed goals, achievements, or skills that clearly refutes this false assumption that others have made about you?

- What do you believe it will take for you to replace these negative, false views of yourself with what God says is true about who you are?

EXPLORING GOD'S WORD

Who you *think* you are drives your behavior. Numerous psychological studies have demonstrated the power of our thoughts to shape our decisions and actions. But our thinking often gets polluted by false labels, biased beliefs, and inaccurate assumptions we absorb from those around us. Unfortunately, we're often inclined to believe, whether consciously or not, what others tell us about our identity, particularly those who have proximity and power in our lives.

The only source you can trust to speak the truth of who you are is your Creator, your Heavenly Father who loved you so much he sent his Son to die for you. From Genesis to Revelation, God's Word reveals who he says you are—his son or daughter created in his divine image (see Genesis 1:26) as well as a new creation and coheir with Christ (see Romans 8:17; 2 Corinthians 5:17).

Just as the false beliefs you hold accumulated and solidified over time, replacing them with God's truth about your identity also takes time. Reading a verse quickly or scanning a familiar passage won't cut it. You need to meditate on the truth of your identity in Scripture. Absorbing the eternal truth of who you are requires chewing on it and digesting it, letting it become central to your thinking, not just another competing voice in your mind.

Toward this goal of letting God's truth about your identity sink in, read the following passage and then answer the questions below.

> [14] *For Christ's love compels us, because we are convinced that one died for all, and therefore all died.* [15] *And he died for all, that those who live should no longer live for themselves but for him who died for them and was raised again.*
>
> [16] *So from now on we regard no one from a worldly point of view. Though we once regarded Christ in this way, we do so no longer.* [17] *Therefore, if anyone is in Christ, the new creation has come: The old has gone, the new is here!*
>
> **2 CORINTHIANS 5:14–17**

- Why does it often seem easier to view ourselves (and others) from a "worldly point of view"? According to 2 Corinthians 5:14–17, why is this perspective no longer accurate or relevant?

- If you have committed your life to Christ, what has changed in your life? How do those changes reflect the new creation you are in Christ?

- Based on your understanding of the passage, what is true about your identity? Why does accepting this truth mean letting go of false beliefs that often poison your mind?

EMBRACING THE TRUTH

In addition to being influenced by what other people think of us, we also tend to define ourselves by our worst moments and habitual sins. For instance, if you frequently struggle with eating healthy and taking care of your body, you might conclude that you're overweight, lazy, and undisciplined. If you rarely seem to handle money well and stay on budget, you might tell yourself that you're a victim of your low-paying job or that you're just not smart enough to be financially responsible.

These extreme labels we give ourselves often echo in our thinking, undermining our efforts, but they are far from true. They do not define who we are, nor do they determine our future. But the devil seizes our self-critical tendencies as opportunities to keep us limited in our ability to see ourselves, our lives, and God clearly and accurately. Your spiritual enemy is real, and he delights in trying to take you out. "Your enemy the devil prowls around like a roaring lion looking for someone to devour" (1 Peter 5:8).

Satan's weapon of choice is usually deception. "When he lies, he speaks his native language, for he is a liar and the father of lies" (John 8:44). His primary target is your identity. Knowing how your self-perception affects your decisions and behavior, he lies to you about who you are. This is the trick he pulls back in tthe Garden of Eden when he says to Eve, "Did God really say, 'You must not eat from any tree in the garden'?" (Genesis 3:1). On the front end, the devil tempts you by questioning and justifying sinful choices. After the fact, he rushes to heap on condemnation to make you feel worse about yourself.

But you are not who the enemy says you are. He is merely "the accuser" (Revelation 12:10). You are who God says you are. Your loving Father offers affirmations, not accusations. Even before you were born, God designed you as his creation; you are "fearfully and wonderfully made" (Psalm 139:14). He knows your worst moments and your best and loves you unconditionally in both. In fact, the one who knows your worst loves you best. Your holy Creator defines the true you.

- What are some of the self-condemning labels you've discovered in your thinking? Which one have you been struggling with most recently?

- How aware have you been of the enemy using your self-critical thoughts against you? What have you done to dispel his deception in order to see yourself clearly?

- Why does it often feel easier to be harshly negative about ourselves than to believe the unerringly positive truth? In other words, why do we tend to trust our own views rather than God's?

- When you think about the very worst moments of your life—times when you've made bad decisions with painful consequences—how does knowing God loves you even in those moments change the way you see yourself?

CHANGING THE WAY YOU CHANGE

It's one thing to know you're clinging to false notions of who you are but another to replace them with the truth of who God declares you to be. At the end of chapter 1.3 in *The Power to Change*, exercise 4 asks you to list the lies, false beliefs, and accusations that have accumulated in your thinking from the unreliable views of others, your own subjective criticism, and the deception of the deceiver.

Then you're told to review the biblical identity statements at the end of chapter 1.3 and identify the one(s) resonating most powerfully.

Now it's time to take this exercise one step further. For this additional step, you will need two pieces of paper, detached and average in size, large enough for you to draw and doodle. On one of them, draw a circle in the center and write, "Who I Think I Am." From this hub, draw lines to other circles and write in the false labels and accusations, both from others and yourself, that you've uncovered. Doodle or draw to illustrate if you feel inspired. Once you've included all the bad stuff you can think of, put this paper aside.

On the other sheet of paper, draw another central circle and write, "Who I Know I Am Because God Says So." Once again, draw extending lines that connect to circles (or stars or whatever you want) that contain the true identity verses from Scripture or one name or truth that summarizes them. Feel free to draw or doodle to further illustrate these facets of your true identity.

Once you've completed both visual depictions, study them for a moment. They're not meant to be works of art or perfect portrayals, so focus instead on what they represent and reveal about who you truly are. Use the questions below to reflect on this activity.

* What stood out or resonated most with you while completing these visuals? Why?

* How does this exercise make you feel about the way you usually see yourself? About the way God sees you?

- What images, doodles, or sketches—if any—did you include? How do these illustrate each particular page?

- Where can you put the page reflecting who God says you are as a reminder to focus on what is true about who you are?

KEEPING THE CHANGE

The good work of transformation that God began in you—his activity of making you complete, steady, strong, and firm—is something that he is doing and will continue to do until his work in you is finally finished (see Philippians 1:6).

You *will* change, and you *can* become who you want to become.

Whoever you want to become, you *can* become that person. And knowing that you are called to more, who you truly are—and who you want to become—is how you begin any successful attempt at change.

You began envisioning the future you in exercise 5 at the end of chapter 1.4 in *The Power to Change.* You were asked to describe the hero you want to be in ten years and then commit that vision to God in prayer. But ten years might seem like a long time from now. You might be tempted to lose sight of your true-identity-based future self. So revisit that exercise, but focus on the better person you want to be one year from now. Use the questions below to help in this exercise as you seek to set goals for becoming all that God has created you to be.

- What three words best describe the future you at exactly this same time next year? How do these descriptors express how you will improve?

- If you were to prioritize things you want to change about yourself, what one change would be at the top of your list? Why?

- In order to see this change occur in your future, what needs to happen? What steps can you take toward making this aspect of your identity shine a year from now?

- Of these steps, which one can you start implementing today? It doesn't have to be big or dramatic—in fact, it may be better if it's not. Ask God to help you follow through this week.

FOCUS ON WHO BEFORE DO

Your calling is more about who you are becoming than what you are doing.

CRAIG GROESCHEL

Imagine being widowed not once but twice before the age of thirty-five. Imagine losing four of your five young children to disease and injury. Imagine being an African American woman lacking formal education in the U.S. during the American Civil War. Imagine having a dream of preaching the gospel not only in your community but overseas.

You only have to consider the life of Amanda Berry Smith to know how radically different your story can be by the time it's finished. Based on circumstances, history, and the world into which she was born, Mrs. Smith could easily have been someone who saw herself as a victim with little chance of change. But Amanda Berry Smith knew she was more than any of the limitations and labels of her circumstances. She let God define her identity and consistently answered the call he placed on her life, improving the lives of countless others and making history in the process.[6]

Born into slavery in 1837, Amanda Berry was soon emancipated when her father purchased his family's freedom—for himself, his wife, and their five children. Amanda received only a few months of formal education—a privilege reserved primarily for white children at the time. She refused to let this fact limit her capacity for learning, however, remaining a lifelong, mostly self-taught student.

Mrs. Smith also refused to allow society and culture to dictate to her who she was and what she could do. At a time when most women were not allowed to lead or speak publicly, Amanda Smith became a preacher, Bible teacher, missionary, and philanthropist, addressing both Black and white audiences. Although not ordained or supported by any denomination or organization, in 1878 she became the first Black woman to serve as an international evangelist—in England, Ireland, Scotland, India, and several African nations.[7]

Returning to the U.S. twelve years later, Mrs. Smith settled in Chicago and founded an orphanage, wrote a monthly newsletter, and published her autobiography before she died in 1915.

Amanda Berry Smith provides a shining example of someone focusing on who God called her to be before doing all he asked her to do. She knew that how her story began didn't have to be how it ended.

- What aspect of Amanda Berry Smith's life stands out to you? Why?

- How would you describe the purpose you believe God has created you to fulfill? What is your basis for this conclusion?

- How are you presently living out your God-given purpose? What is standing in your way or impeding your progress?

- How have you defied social and cultural expectations to obey God's call on your life?

EXPLORING GOD'S WORD

If you've ever longed for more in your life—more meaning, more peace, more fulfillment—it's likely because God calls you to more. While the world around you pushes money, fame, social media celebrity, and possessions, God created you with unique gifts to serve the purpose for which he made you. His "more" is the only more that satisfies. Scripture urges you "to lead a life worthy of your calling, for you have been called by God" (Ephesians 4:1 NLT).

Most people associate *doing* something with being called by God. They wonder what job, ministry, or relationships he's directing them toward and where they should go in response. Some people even fear that they might not hear God's calling. But we often have it backward when it comes to our understanding of our calling. Throughout the Bible it's clear that God's calling focuses on who we *are* before what we *do*.

One of the most dramatic examples of this sequence comes from the testimony of the apostle Paul. He doesn't start out as an apostle or as Paul. While hunting down Jesus' followers to imprison them, Saul (as he was then known) is confronted by Jesus himself, and the encounter leaves him temporarily blinded.

It seems safe to say that Saul has no idea of his true identity or his divine purpose until he experiences God's calling on his life. Read through the passage below describing his experience, and then answer the questions that follow.

> [1] *Meanwhile, Saul was still breathing out murderous threats against the Lord's disciples. He went to the high priest* [2] *and asked him for letters to the synagogues in Damascus, so that if he found any there who belonged to the Way, whether men or women, he might take them as prisoners to Jerusalem.* [3] *As he neared Damascus on his journey, suddenly a light from heaven flashed around him.* [4] *He fell to the ground and heard a voice say to him, "Saul, Saul, why do you persecute me?"*
>
> [5] *"Who are you, Lord?" Saul asked.*
>
> *"I am Jesus, whom you are persecuting," he replied.* [6] *"Now get up and go into the city, and you will be told what you must do."*
>
> ACTS 9:1–6

● How was Saul's view of his identity and purpose almost opposite of the way God saw him? What does this reveal about the way God calls us still today?

● Why is Saul's question, "Who are you, Lord?" foundational to knowing who you are called to be? How does knowing who God is determine your understanding of who you are?

- Why was it essential for Saul to be stopped in his tracks in order to be redirected by God's calling? When has God brought you to a halt in order to reinforce his calling?

- What does it mean for you to "lead a life worthy of your calling" (Ephesians 4:1 NLT)? What has this looked like so far?

EMBRACING THE TRUTH

When you have clarity about the unique way in which God made you, you will begin to understand what God has for you to do. *Who* comes before *do*. Foremost, God has called you to a holy life, to be faithful to him, to realize that nothing else compares to "the surpassing worth of knowing Christ Jesus" (Philippians 3:8). You become a new creation in Christ before you fully discover what you're created to do.

What you're called to do might feel small—especially when compared to others doing dramatic deeds—but nothing you do is small when you know who you're called to be. "And whatever you do, whether in word or deed, do it all in the name of the Lord Jesus, giving thanks to God the Father through him" (Colossians 3:17).

After his stunning conversion, Saul realized that he wasn't who he thought he was. As a devoted follower of Jesus committed to sharing the good news of the gospel message, he discovered what he needed to do. Read the conclusion of his initial transformation and answer the remaining questions.

[17] Then Ananias went to the house and entered it. Placing his hands on Saul, he said, "Brother Saul, the Lord—Jesus, who appeared to you on the road as you were coming here—has sent me so that you may see again and be filled with the Holy Spirit." [18] Immediately, something like scales fell from Saul's eyes, and he could see again. He got up and was baptized, [19] and after taking some food, he regained his strength.

Saul spent several days with the disciples in Damascus. [20] At once he began to preach in the synagogues that Jesus is the Son of God.

ACTS 9:17-20

- When have you focused more on what you were doing for God than on who you are in Christ? What were the consequences?

- What does Saul's blindness and subsequent sight restoration symbolize to you? Why?

- When have you failed to see who you are and consequently failed to do what you're uniquely called to do?

- What is one aspect of your calling that you're already living out? How does it reflect who God made you to be?

CHANGING THE WAY YOU CHANGE

The usual progression of spiritual growth and personal change begins with salvation, followed by sanctification, then by knowing how you're called to serve. At the end of chapter 1.5, exercise 6 instructed you to describe each of these three phases in your own life. While you may have focused at times on one of these, you may not have taken in all three and their interconnected relationship. Taking a look at the big picture of your life, however, is essential if you're going to access God's power and experience lasting change.

So now take exercise 6 one step further by examining the relationships among your salvation, your sanctification, and your service. While one or more may be easy to delineate, they often overlap throughout your lifetime spiritual journey. One may seem based in a specific event, place, and time, while another might be more ambiguous, ongoing, and elusive. When you see how all three relate, though, you often gain a clearer sense of your identity and purpose. Knowing your *who* before your *do* is foundational to the power to change.

With this goal in mind, answer the following questions.

SALVATION

- How has your perspective on your personal faith testimony changed from the time you began following Jesus?

- Was your desire to change aspects of your life part of the motivation to become a believer? If so, what aspects in particular?

- How has your salvation experience overlapped with your sanctification?

SANCTIFICATION

- Review the list of significant changes you made in exercise 6. What patterns of personal change stand out?

- What changes have not yet happened as you hoped when you became a believer?

- How has your relationship with God changed the most since you became a Christian?

SERVICE

- How does your calling to serve overlap with how you've changed since following Christ? What changes have taken place in you that facilitate what you're called to do?

- In other words, how have aspects of your *do* emerged from your *who*?

- What do you believe God has called you to do that is still in process?

KEEPING THE CHANGE

Discovering your calling and living out your purpose can sometimes feel like a lifelong process. Even after God has placed a call on your life and guided you to serve, you may still struggle to experience a sense of divine fulfillment—a confidence that you're doing what you were created to do. While their identity remains the same, many people see the *do* part of their calling expressed in ways that evolve and change over their lifetime. Look back on your life and reflect on how you have ended up doing what you're doing now. Ask God to open your eyes and heart to help you discern a deeper, clearer sense of how he made you and what he wants you to do next. Use the questions below to assist in your reflection.

- After calling Jesus his Lord, Saul's name in Scripture is changed to Paul. If you were to be given a new name by God that reflects your *who*, what would it be? Why?

- On a scale of 1 to 10, with 1 being "totally uncertain" and 10 being "absolutely certain," how confident are you that you're living out your calling?

- What gives you the most joy when serving others? When do you feel most alive, excited, and eager to serve?

- How is this personal passion expressed in your actions? How do you usually feel about doing what you believe God created you to do?

- Fill in the blanks: "My purpose in life is _____, and I know this because _____."

PART 2

TRAINING. NOT TRYING.

A s you saw in section 1, in order to experience lasting change, you need to think the right thoughts about yourself, know your true identity, and start your identity with *who*, not *do*. The next step is determining what your goal is and what a win looks like for this goal. This process can happen in many ways, but it often becomes an action point when pain, crisis, or conflict arises. You don't need to wait until you're hurting to begin, which is why it's important to focus on *training*, not *trying*. Here's how:

- Defining your win is how you begin.
- Trying doesn't work. Training does.
- Trying is an attempt to do the right thing by exerting effort in the moment.
- Training is a commitment to strategic habits you do before the moment that equip you to do the right thing in the moment.
- Discipline is choosing what you want most over what you want now.
- The path to public success is always paved with private discipline.
- Make doing your habit your win.
- You don't have to win every day to win.
- It's time to define your win so you can quit trying and begin training.

TRYING VS. TRAINING

Keep practicing your strategic habits,
and you will reach your goal. . . .
Trying tends to be a momentary reaction,
while training is an ongoing action.

CRAIG GROESCHEL

Winning an Olympic gold medal requires more than just wanting to win and showing up for the race. Regardless of the sporting event, grabbing the gold on the world stage of the Olympics means training as a lifestyle. Most athletes consider it a career-defining achievement just to participate in the Olympic Games. Most have been training almost all their lives.

This is certainly the case for the most decorated Olympian of all time, superstar swimmer Michael Phelps. With a total of twenty-eight medals, Phelps holds all-time records in numerous individual and team trials and events across five different Olympic Games. He began swimming when he was seven and within a few years displayed the raw talent and trainability of a champion.[8]

But many people consider Phelps an even greater champion because of his willingness to reveal his years-long battle with depression, anxiety, and suicidal thoughts. As surprising as it may seem, all the training, all the victories, all the medals weren't enough for Phelps to feel mentally healthy and whole. When faced with his second DUI in 2014, Michael Phelps reached a breaking point. "I felt like I didn't want to be alive anymore," he admits, acknowledging his awareness of how much he was hurting and disappointing others.[9]

After wrestling with what he should do for several days, Phelps says, "I then just decided that it was time to take a step to try to find a different route, a different path." He then checked into an in-patient recovery and treatment center for forty-five days. In interviews afterward, Phelps has consistently revealed that mental health is a process that requires flexibility, comparing the pursuit of mental strength to the physical training required to be the best swimmer in the world. "I'm constantly learning. I'm constantly growing," he shares.[10]

- What assumptions do you make about people who succeed at a high level? Why do we often assume superstars rarely struggle?

- What is a goal that you have repeatedly *tried* to achieve rather than *trained* to achieve? What have you learned from this pursuit?

- How have you experienced the difference between trying and training in the past? How would you describe the distinction between them?

- When have you trained to reach a goal, such as running a 10K, hiking a particular trail, or finishing a degree or certification? How would you describe your training process in fulfilling this particular goal?

EXPLORING GOD'S WORD

You don't have to consider yourself athletically inclined to appreciate, admire, and respect the training, discipline, and drive of world-class athletes like Michael Phelps. Perhaps you have a favorite sport and enjoy keeping up with its stars and standouts. You might have even played this sport when you were in school, or you're coaching your kids in it now. Regardless of the sport, you have likely observed what elite athletes and serious fans know: no matter how much natural talent someone has, if they don't train, they don't win.

The apostle Paul drew on this same kind of cultural knowledge in a letter he wrote to believers in the early church at Corinth, a city in Greece. Written around AD 55, what we now call 1 Corinthians demonstrates Paul's knowledge of his audience. Every four years from 776 BC to AD 393, the ancient Olympic Games were held in Olympia, the city which gave the competition the name we still use today.

Corinth was home to a similar recurring event known as the Isthmian Games, usually occurring each year before and after the Olympic Games. With these competitions in mind, Paul knew the Corinthians would find his metaphor, which you'll find in the passage below, accessible and familiar. Read through it and then answer the questions that follow.

> [24] *Don't you realize that in a race everyone runs, but only one person gets the prize? So run to win!* [25] *All athletes are disciplined in their training. They do it to win a prize that will fade away, but we do it for an eternal prize.* [26] *So I run with purpose in every step. I am not just shadowboxing.* [27] *I discipline my body like an athlete, training it to do what it should. Otherwise, I fear that after preaching to others I myself might be disqualified.*
>
> **1 CORINTHIANS 9:24–27 NLT**

- What do you believe generally motivates elite athletes? Money, awards, fame, something else?

- How competitive do you consider yourself? What do you enjoy doing just for the sheer pleasure of it?

- What stands out to you in Paul's comparison? What does it mean to race for a prize that will not fade away?

- How is *trying* similar to what Paul calls "shadowboxing" (verse 26)? How is *training* similar to running "with purpose in every step"?

EMBRACING THE TRUTH

Paul's letter to the Corinthians is not the only time we find athletic metaphors in Scripture. Hebrews 12 begins with a similar comparison and circles back to it toward the end of the chapter. Once again, our spiritual life is compared to running a race that requires ongoing training. We're reminded that following Jesus is not a one-time decision but the process of salvation, sanctification, and serving covered in lesson 3. As you read through the verses below, underline or circle any words or phrases that stand out to you, then answer the questions that follow.

> [1] *Therefore, since we are surrounded by such a huge crowd of witnesses to the life of faith, let us strip off every weight that slows us down, especially the sin that so easily trips us up. And let us run with endurance the race God has set before us.* [2] *We do this by keeping our eyes on Jesus, the champion who initiates and perfects our faith....*

*12 So take a new grip with your tired hands and strengthen your weak knees.
13 Mark out a straight path for your feet so that those who are weak and lame will
not fall but become strong.*

HEBREWS 12:1–2, 12–13 NLT

- What is different about this passage's running metaphor compared to the metaphor in 1 Corinthians? What does each passage emphasize?

- What sins have tripped you up as you've run the race God has set before you (see verse 1)? How have you previously tried to eliminate these weights that slow down your progress?

- How does keeping your eyes on Jesus motivate you to persevere in the race of faith? How does his example motivate you in the way you live each day?

- What words or phrases did you underline or circle in this passage? Why do you think they resonate with you right now?

CHANGING THE WAY YOU CHANGE

Goals give direction. Without direction, you're running a race with no finish line. It may be tempting to define your win like most people in the culture define winning: making more money, achieving more accolades, showing off purchases and exclusive vacations. But chasing these goals means you're losing sight of your own finish lines. You're allowing others to determine what you want and how to achieve it—and this won't work for sustaining real change. You want your goals to be specifically yours.

Surveying all areas of your life and the wins you want can be overwhelming. You're not sure where to start and how to proceed to accomplish any one of them, let alone all of them, which is why it's vitally important to prioritize and to scale specific goals around doable habits and practices. If you haven't already chosen one area as your primary focus, now is the time. No matter how many things you would love to change and how many goals you want to achieve, starting with one makes it manageable—something you can begin right away, right now.

Toward that goal, review your answers to exercise 8 at the end of chapter 2.1 in *The Power to Change*. Then use the questions below to help you clarify and strategize how you will begin training for your specific win.

- When you look back at exercise 8, what is the primary area you want to focus on first? Why?

- With this area in mind, think back on what you've tried before that hasn't worked or lasted. How can you train toward your win rather than merely trying again?

- What exactly do you envision when you consider your win in this primary area of change? Close your eyes for a few moments and turn your imagination loose, and then describe what you see.

- Training involves practicing over and over again as you master certain skills and abilities. With your primary goal in mind, what is one small habit or practice you can begin today?

KEEPING THE CHANGE

Many people want to train but can't shake their "try" mindset. They often attempt practices and habits that are out of reach based on where they are. The best trainers usually start small while thinking big. They realize they can't take giant steps to cross their finish line, so they break down their training journey into smaller, bite-sized pieces.

One effective way to begin might surprise you: imagine taking your goal to an extreme level, and then work backward. If you make your goal an impossible dream, you can work backward until you find a way to train that is doable today.

For example, you know you want to run more often because you enjoy it as a way to exercise and get healthy. But each morning you hit snooze rather than getting up early to jog before work. Each afternoon and evening, the gravity of your weary day pulls you to your couch. Completing a 10K is something you've always wanted to do, but it remains out of reach because you don't run regularly.

So instead of a 10K, imagine your goal is now to run a marathon—no, not just any marathon, but the *Boston Marathon* or the *New York Marathon*. Sounds impossible, right? But if that were your goal, what could you do *today* so that next year you would be closer to running in the Boston Marathon?

For starters, you could walk more places, perhaps park farther away from your destinations to get in a few more steps. You could create a new playlist and find a couple podcasts to listen to while you go for a walk in your neighborhood after work. You could see how your running shoes are holding up and do some online research into the best brand for your needs.

- Okay, now it's your turn to do this "impossible dream" exercise. Use the questions and prompts below to help you think through how to get going toward your win. Complete the following: When I imagine taking my goal to an "impossible" extreme, I think of _____.

- Working backward from this seemingly impossible goal, what are some major milestone accomplishment goals along the way? (For example, if you decided running in the Boston Marathon was your impossible goal, then running in a 5K, 10K, and 25K might be smaller milestones to train toward.)

- Fill in the blanks: The main reason I cannot see myself ever doing or completing (insert your impossible dream here) _____ _____ is because _____ _____.

- One way to overcome or at least chip away at this excuse would be to start _____
  _____
  _____ .

- What are three bite-sized baby steps you can begin right away toward your (no longer so impossible) goal? For now, start as small as you can imagine.

GRATIFICATION VS. DISCIPLINE

Discipline is choosing what you want most over what you want now.

CRAIG GROESCHEL

You may have heard of the marshmallow experiment, a series of studies in the early 1970s conducted by Walter Mischel, a psychology professor at Stanford University. Mischel and his team tested several hundred children individually, mostly aged four to five, by offering them a simple but intriguing deal. The tester presented each kid with a marshmallow, which they could eat while the tester stepped out of the room for a while (usually about fifteen minutes), or they could wait until the tester returned and be given a second marshmallow. Basically, they could eat one now or two later.

While the results proved insightful, it was the follow-up study on the participants that was even more revealing. "The researchers followed each child for more than 40 years," explains author James Clear, "and over and over again, the group who waited patiently for the second marshmallow succeeded in whatever capacity they were measuring. In other words, this series of experiments proved that the ability to delay gratification was critical for success in life."[11]

The children who deferred gratification in the original experiments used a variety of instinctive strategies to resist temptation. Some closed their eyes or turned their back on the marshmallow before them. Others sang to themselves or played with their fingers and toes—basically, whatever it took to distract themselves from wanting the one marshmallow right then when they could have two later. Journalist Janine Zacharia concludes, "These studies demystified willpower and showed how self-control and emotion regulation could be enhanced, taught and learned, beginning very early in life, even by children who initially had much difficulty delaying gratification."[12]

Which is good news for you as you redefine self-discipline.

* When you were a child, would you likely have chosen the one marshmallow right away or waited to have two? What makes you think so?

* Do you generally think of yourself as a person with strong self-discipline? Based on what?

- What areas of your life are more disciplined than others? What do you think makes the difference?

- What is one of your marshmallows that is often hard to resist? Chocolate? Online shopping? Microbrew beverages? Something else?

EXPLORING GOD'S WORD

For followers of Jesus, spiritual growth requires discipline. As you begin to put sin behind you, develop and mature in your faith, serve and achieve for God's kingdom, you must give up certain things and embrace others. Basically, any growth experience in which you become stronger, wiser, and more capable relies on this building block of lasting change—discipline.

You might have an immediate reaction or aversion to the idea of discipline. You may hold an extreme perspective on discipline because of past conditioning and learning. You might recall times when you've failed to follow through or been unable to resist temptation. Perhaps you associate discipline with forcing yourself to give up things you love and to do things you hate. Maybe you've concluded you're just not a disciplined kind of person.

But discipline gets a bad rap. In order to experience lasting change, discipline is inevitable—but it doesn't have to be despicable. Instead of whatever comes to your mind now, consider owning a new definition of discipline: *discipline is choosing what you want most over what you want now*. To help that sink in, read the passage below and answer the questions that follow.

16 Therefore we do not lose heart. Though outwardly we are wasting away, yet inwardly we are being renewed day by day. 17 For our light and momentary troubles are achieving for us an eternal glory that far outweighs them all. 18 So we fix our eyes not on what is seen, but on what is unseen, since what is seen is temporary, but what is unseen is eternal.

2 CORINTHIANS 4:16–18

- What are your usual associations, thoughts, and feelings related to discipline? What sources and experiences have influenced these default associations?

- Do you agree that discipline is essential for spiritual growth? How have you experienced this in your own faith journey?

- What sinful habits and worldly pleasures have you given up since becoming a follower of Jesus? Which ones still tempt or ensnare you?

- What is your takeaway from this passage of Scripture? How does changing your focus automatically help change your understanding of discipline?

EMBRACING THE TRUTH

There's always something you want *now*—more money, homemade cheesecake, a new iPhone, pro golf clubs, a beachside villa, or that designer outfit you can't afford. While many of these wants may be out of reach, the *now* desire you experience remains powerful and seductive. It promises instant gratification but rarely satisfies for very long.

There is also something you want *most*—a stronger marriage, healthy relationships with your kids, a stronger body, to be debt-free, a deep and abiding faith in God. Your *most* desire rarely provides instant gratification. It requires a slower, more incremental process over time. But it offers you something far more important—the life you want to live. Discipline is choosing what you want most over what you want now.

The bottom line is you can't avoid pain.

It's either the pain of discipline now or the pain of regret later.

- As you consider the kind of pain you want to endure, it might be helpful to compare what you want now with what you want most. Personalize the lists below, being as honest and specific as possible, and then answer the questions that follow.

What I want now	What I want most

- What *now* item promises the quickest gratification? How often do you give in to temptation when this item presents itself?

- How would you describe the pain you've experienced from the times you've chosen the instant gratification of a *now* item?

- What *most* item holds the strongest pull on your heart presently? Why?

- What kind of discipline is required in order to pursue this *most* item?

CHANGING THE WAY YOU CHANGE

Immediate gratification seems easier than discipline when faced with temptation and wanting what you want now. Sure, it temporarily seems easier to choose what you want now, but you live the life you want by choosing what you want most. Training instead of trying means choosing discipline. Discipline means choosing what you want *most* over what you want *now*.

To experience real and lasting change, to finally live the life you want, you want to choose discipline consistently in the moments that matter. But it's painful because you're deferring temporary comfort, pleasure, relief, and fulfillment. Consider how you'll feel afterward, though. Consider why you want to change in the first place. Perhaps because you long for more, for strength and substance over immediate pleasure, for a lifestyle that is fully aligned with your beliefs, values, and faith. Because you're tired of feeling disappointed, embarrassed, ashamed, and regretful.

So accept that there's pain either way—but you can choose which kind of pain you experience. "No discipline is enjoyable while it is happening—it's painful! But afterward there will be a peaceful harvest of right living for those who are trained in this way" (Hebrews 12:11 NLT). To help you compare these two kinds of pain, answer the following questions.

- Do you agree that pain is inevitable in order to experience lasting change? How would you describe the two kinds of pain involved in the struggle between gratification and discipline?

- When have you recently chosen immediate gratification only to regret your choice later? Is the pain of your regret tied to similar choices you've made like this one?

- When have you recently chosen to experience the pain of resisting immediate gratification? Looking back, do you regret that choice now? Explain your response.

- Does remembering what you want most help you resist the temptation to go for what you want now? Why or why not?

KEEPING THE CHANGE

Discipline may feel painful, but if you don't live a disciplined life, you will experience the pain of regret. Not choosing what you want now feels painful. But if you do choose what you want now, you will later experience the pain of not having what you want most.

Pain along the way is far preferable to getting down the road and realizing you missed out on some important aspect of the life God had for you. Desire alone won't get you what you want most, but discipline will. So don't avoid the pain of discipline. If you do, not getting what you want most will be your biggest regret.

Review your answers to exercise 10 at the end of chapter 2.3 in *The Power to Change*. Reflect on what specific habits and choices require discipline on a regular, perhaps daily, basis in order for you to experience lasting change and get what you want most. To help you be mindful of your most when faced in the moment of choosing now, create a way to hit pause so you can focus on what you're gaining in the long term because of what you're giving up short term.

For example, you've decided that you are not a disciplined eater. You realized that if you don't eat your usual bedtime bowl of ice cream, you will lose weight and be healthier. Being mindful of your lighter, healthier body can help you in the moment when you're craving Chunky Monkey. So maybe you put a sticky note with Hebrews 12:11 written on it on your freezer door. When you reach for your fix, it can remind you to give up the pleasurable taste of comfort food now because you're setting your sights on accomplishing something you want more.

Okay, now it's your turn to get creative. How can you hit pause in the moment to activate the discipline necessary to reach your greater goal? Use the questions and prompts below to help you create and position your *hit pause* reminder.

- Which habit, pattern, or choice do you want to work on hitting pause on in order to resist your *now* for your *most*?

- When do you usually face opportunity, inclination, or temptation most for this area you want to work on? Any common factors (your mood, stress level, workload, etc.)?

- What would be the long-term benefit of resisting gratification in this area now? What would you experience, accomplish, or achieve by focusing on what you want most?

Finally, reflect for a few moments on creating a reminder to hit pause in this area. You might decide to write a note to yourself, print a Bible verse on an index card, create a playlist, text a friend for accountability, or place a symbolic item within sight. Choose the reminder that is sure to help you realign your focus. Then use it!

LOSING VS. WINNING

With a training-not-trying approach, you make doing your habit your win.

CRAIG GROESCHEL

Winning is about process, not perfection.

Dick Hoyt, a family man and retired lieutenant colonel in the Air National Guard, discovered this truth in 1977 when his fifteen-year-old son Rick asked if they could run a charity 5K to benefit an injured classmate. Then thirty-six, Dick didn't consider himself a runner, but that wasn't their biggest challenge. His son had been born with severe spastic quadriplegia and Cerebral Palsy, rendering him nonverbal and dependent on a wheelchair for mobility.[13]

But Rick had already defied the odds and overcome greater challenges, learning to communicate via new technology and attending public school after his mother helped to get a special-education bill passed. So running a race seemed doable to both father and son. Pushing Rick in a specially modified wheelchair, Team Hoyt (as they became known) completed that first race—and went on to finish more than 1,000 race events, including seventy-two marathons (they ran the Boston Marathon thirty-two times), and six Ironman Triathlons.[14]

Dick's love for his son obviously motivated the success of Team Hoyt, but clearly he had to change his definition of winning. Rick had reframed winning after that very first race: "Dad, when I'm running, it feels like I'm not handicapped."[15]

- Considering your past goals and achievements, when has winning focused on the process more than the finish line?

- When have you faced a daunting obstacle but refused to let it keep you from your goal? How did you overcome that obstacle?

- What stands out to you about the success of Team Hoyt? Why?

- How did focusing on the process become the Hoyts' win throughout all those race events?

EXPLORING GOD'S WORD

Perhaps it's only human nature that many people's notion of winning tilts toward the hopeful expectation expressed by Jesus's disciples James and John. They ask their Master if he will grant them a favor. When Jesus asks them to disclose the favor, they reply, "Let one of us sit at your right and the other at your left in your glory" (Mark 10:37).

Christ tells them that they don't know what they're asking. Their understanding of power, leadership, and winning, based on an earthly perspective, wasn't the same as God's version. Nonetheless, the matter isn't finished because the rest of the disciples hear what James and John request. So Jesus makes it even clearer to all of them:

> [41] *When the ten heard about this, they became indignant with James and John.* [42] *Jesus called them together and said, "You know that those who are regarded as rulers of the Gentiles lord it over them, and their high officials exercise authority over them.* [43] *Not so with you. Instead, whoever wants to become great among you must be your servant,* [44] *and whoever wants to be first must be slave of all.* [45] *For even the Son of Man did not come to be served, but to serve, and to give his life as a ransom for many."*
>
> **MARK 10:41–45**

- Can you identify with James and John's desire to win and be recognized for it? What do you think motivated their request?

- How does the world define winning? How do contemporary leaders use their wins to "lord it over" others?

- What does it mean that in order to be great, you must become a servant? What does this kind of greatness look like in your life?

- What was Jesus saying when he indicated that winning requires you to lose ambition and embrace service?

EMBRACING THE TRUTH

Winning is not what you think it is.

Most of the time, you've probably focused only on results, on your finish line, on the *after* pic rather than the *before*. One of several problems with this viewpoint is that it shifts your focus from the present to the future. "Once I lose twenty pounds," you tell yourself, "then I'll feel good about myself." "If I ever get out of debt, that is when I'll know I'm a success." "After I've been praying and reading the Bible every day for a year, then I'll know what it takes to be a good Christian."

But based on where you are, what is required to reach those goals often seems too big. Because you can't reach your goal quickly, you're tempted not to even try. This all-or-nothing conditional thinking overlooks the real secret to winning: showing up in the present for the process.

You win when you make *doing* your habit your win.

With a training-not-trying approach, you choose strategic habits, and you consider every day you engage in your process a win. If you focus on your big goal, more often than not, you will feel like you are losing. But if you focus on your habit, you can win every day. Acting on this one shift in perspective can turn your attempts to change upside down.

Accomplishing your goal could take a few years.

But you can do your habits every day.

This truth isn't just a matter of opinion—it's biblical. Jesus says, "Whoever can be trusted with very little can also be trusted with much, and whoever is dishonest with very little will also be dishonest with much" (Luke 16:10).

- When have you fallen into all-or-nothing conditional thinking about a big goal? How did you let the gap between where you were and where the goal was prevent you from training?

- What are habits or routines that you follow most every day? Think about how you eat, sleep, work, play, and travel. What are the benefits of these everyday habits and routines?

- Why is a *training* mindset rather than a *trying* mindset required in order to make doing your habit your win?

- How does doing your habits every day make you a winner regardless of the ultimate outcome?

CHANGING THE WAY YOU CHANGE

Recovery programs sometimes encourage participants to "make the next right choice." The focus is taken off how long it will take to reach your big goal and instead placed on what can be done now. It can be daunting to see how far you are from your goal. So instead, just look at the next step. King Solomon observes, "Patience is better than pride" (Ecclesiastes 7:8).

Patience allows you to sustain your habits rather than to anticipate boasting about your accomplishments. When you make doing the habit your win, you can win with each step you make, each pound you lose, each dollar you pay, each choice you make that eventually leads to your goal. But it starts right now, which is why it's important to think through the habits required to sustain your process-focused win.

With implementing doable daily habits as your goal, complete the following questions and prompts.

- My primary goal right now is _____,
  and some habits that would contribute toward this goal include:

- Of these potential new habits, which one do you anticipate being the easiest to implement right away? Why?

- Which habits seem too hard or complicated considering your life right now? Why?

- The habit that I feel drawn to begin practicing is _____.

KEEPING THE CHANGE

"I'm in training" is an important phrase for change.

Why? Because it keeps you focused on the process, on doing your habits. You consistently engage in your strategic routines, taking each step as it comes, day by day. You haven't yet achieved your goal. But you continue to pursue with purpose, proclaiming, "I'm in training." No one—especially you—expects perfection or a giant stride overnight.

Winning is about your process, not perfection. You're a winner because you're training, not because of whether or when you reach your big goal. This connects back to the *who before do* idea that identity drives behavior.

When you're trying, it's like you keep hoping to become something you're not. But when you're training, you keep getting better at what you already are! You're not trying—you're in training. Training isn't about being perfect or believing you have to get it right every time. No, the emphasis is on showing up, on practice, on doing what you've decided your training entails.

What exactly *does* your training involve? What are the habits you want to practice regardless of how you feel or the chaotic circumstances around you? Write your answers below and get ready to train like you've never trained before!

- My training includes the following habit(s):

- The habit(s) I'm committing to practice every day in order to win are:

- Knowing what has hindered and derailed my attempts in the past, this time I will not allow _____
to prevent me from practicing my habit(s) and enjoying my daily win.

PART 3

HABITS. NOT HOPE.

The secret to lasting change is not what you hope for—it's the habits you do. The small things no one sees can lead to the big results everyone wants. A habit is basically behavioral autopilot. You already have dozens of habits, perhaps without recognizing them as habits! Experiencing the power of lasting change requires learning to identify and readjust your habits, breaking the ones that aren't good for you and implementing others that allow you to change and thrive. Here are the main principles for part 3:

- If you want to change who you're becoming, change your habits.
- If you want to change where you're going, change your habits.
- If you want to change your life, change your habits.
- Never underestimate how God can start something big through one small habit.
- The small things no one sees can lead to the big results everyone wants.
- Success happens not by accident but by habits.
- A habit is behavioral autopilot born of the process of cue, craving, response, and reward.
- Make your habit obvious, attractive, easy, communal, and repetitious.
- Good habits are difficult to start because the pain comes now and the payoff is in the future.
- Bad habits are difficult to stop because the payoff comes now and the pain is in the future.
- Success is becoming more like Jesus.

SMALL HABITS AND BIG CHANGES

*Your choices create the course and contours of your life.
Your decisions determine your destiny. And your choices are
less intentional and more habitual than you realize.*

CRAIG GROESCHEL

World records are often the result of one person's passion for a particular activity, event, or item. What starts small soon becomes their thing, and then the next thing they know they're going for a world record. Until the next person breaks that record.

Curiously enough, the undisputed keeper of world records started out much the same way. When Sir Hugh Beaver was managing director of the renowned Guinness Brewery in Dublin during the 1950s, he found himself in an argument without resolution. As part of a shooting party in the Irish countryside, Sir Hugh and his hosts began discussing what the fastest game bird in Europe was. They began consulting various reference books without finding a definitive answer.

This incident inspired Sir Hugh with a promotional idea for the Guinness Brewery: to compile a book of facts, dates, and figures that could be used to settle pub arguments. So in 1954, he hired two brothers, Norris and Ross McWhirter, to conduct research and bring his idea to life. Needing to be updated on a regular basis, the *Guinness Book of Records* mushroomed into the iconic resource it's become today, "the ultimate authority on record-breaking achievements."

All because some Irishmen couldn't agree on which game bird was fastest.[16]

- If you were to attempt a world record, what would it be for? Why that feat?

- When have you started something—a hobby, a favor for a friend, a trip, a curiosity—that blossomed into a larger passion? How would you describe the process?

- Based on how often you do it, what is one habit that qualifies you as an expert? Meditating? Writing thank you cards? Recycling? Paying bills? Something else?

● What is the healthiest or best habit you've been doing the longest? What started you doing it?

EXPLORING GOD'S WORD

Think of something you do almost every day, such as flossing, driving to work, cooking dinner, putting your kids to bed, walking the dog, watching TV. Now think about doing this activity today or the most recent time you did it. Can you remember what you were wearing, whom you saw, what was said, or what you watched? With routine habits that are regularly part of your day, you likely shift into autopilot at some point while you're doing it.

In fact, much of what you do on any given day is not the result of your conscious choices as much as your daily habits. Studies have shown that as much as 40 percent of the actions people perform during an average day are based on their habits.[17] You do so much of what you do because it's what you almost always do.

Consider the impact of this phenomenon for a moment. If your decisions determine your destiny, and you're not making all of them, then your destiny suddenly relies on your ongoing habits. Even what you consider daily choices—what to wear, where to park, what to eat, what to do after work—are less intentional and more habitual than you probably realize.

Now that you're focusing on the power to change, it's time to focus on the power your habits have on your life, for better and for worse. Greater still, it's time to be more deliberate about what you allow to become a habit. With this goal in mind, read this passage from Romans and answer the questions that follow.

> [15] *I don't really understand myself, for I want to do what is right, but I don't do it. Instead, I do what I hate.* [16] *But if I know that what I am doing is wrong, this shows that I agree that the law is good.* [17] *So I am not the one doing wrong; it is sin*

living in me that does it. [18] *And I know that nothing good lives in me, that is, in my sinful nature. I want to do what is right, but I can't.* [19] *I want to do what is good, but I don't. I don't want to do what is wrong, but I do it anyway.*

ROMANS 7:15–19 NLT

- What percentage of your day do you believe you operate on habitually based auto-pilot? What are a few of the activities you know you usually do without consciously choosing to do so?

- Compare your bad habits to your good habits. Which outweighs the other? Why do you think this is the case?

- When was the last time you felt the kind of frustration Paul describes in this passage? What were the circumstances?

- When have you been motivated to eliminate a bad habit in your life? What was the catalyst for this elimination?

EMBRACING THE TRUTH

If you take a good hard look at your past efforts to change, you may notice that your hope usually eclipsed your habits. You held high hopes for the changes you wanted to see, but your follow-through fell apart somewhere. It's easy to hope you lose weight, get your promotion, improve your marriage, or grow stronger in your faith. But doing what it takes to make any of those a reality requires training. And training requires habits. Hope in and of itself is not a strategy.

You have not gotten where you are right now because of hope. You are largely who and where you are because of your habits. In order to experience lasting change, you must master the habits that matter most. Changing your habits allows you to change who you're becoming, where you're going, and how you live your life. Habits are often small actions with big consequences.

Never underestimate how God can start something big through one small habit: "If you are faithful in little things, you will be faithful in large ones" (Luke 16:10 NLT). The small things no one sees can lead to the big results everyone wants. Your success happens not by accident but by habits.

- When was the last time you hoped for a change in your life without following through or taking action?

- What does it usually take to motivate you to begin a new healthy habit? Do you need a specific catalyst, or do you just decide and begin doing it? Explain your response.

- What specific habits have served you well so far in your life? Don't overlook even basic ones such as brushing your teeth, flossing, staying hydrated, having your car's oil changed regularly, and so on.

- Think about one negative or harmful habit that remains a struggle for you. How did it begin? What prompted you to continue doing it until it became a habit?

CHANGING THE WAY YOU CHANGE

In exercise 13 at the end of chapter 3.1 in *The Power to Change*, you were asked to examine an average day and note your usual habits and routines, including ones you usually do without having to think. Go back and review what you listed and add anything else that you've thought of since you did it. Try to be as objective as possible in reviewing these habits and routines in order to evaluate your personal strengths and weaknesses when it comes to habits in your life. Use the questions below to facilitate your analysis.

- What time of day appears to be your most productive? Your least?

- What part of your day seems to lack regular habits and routines? What happens during that part of an average day?

- What habit or routine surprises you the most on your list? Why?

- What habit or routine makes you feel pleased, proud, or grateful? Which one leaves you feeling discouraged, disappointed, or frustrated?

KEEPING THE CHANGE

You always have the ability to choose and to choose differently than you've chosen before. You are not a victim of your circumstances or the decisions and actions of others. You are not a passive participant in your life—if you want a big change, then start small. You don't have to keep hoping for change, because you have the ability to start and maintain habits that will bring the changes you want to see.

You'll recall from reading chapter 3.2 in *The Power to Change* that often one small habit can have a domino effect, leading to better choices and healthier habits. These are sometimes called "keystone habits" and serve as crucial building blocks in your journey to change. They set you up for success because they reinforce the training and discipline required for lasting change. They remind you that you are more than capable of controlling your habits intentionally and exercising the self-discipline required to sustain your training.

Review exercise 13 once again, and then complete a similar schedule for your average day below—only this time focus on your ability to choose which habits to keep and which new ones to add. This new, revised version should not be your ideal day or a perfectly balanced schedule because you never know what disruptions or surprises any given day may hold. With this in mind, you might decide to drop only one habit and add another in its place. Or you might use that one habit to ripple into your other habits and routines for the rest of your day.

Morning:

Midday:

Afternoon:

Nighttime:

START THIS AND STOP THAT

If you want to start a new habit, make it obvious.

CRAIG GROESCHEL

If you've ever had a pet, you've probably observed firsthand the way that animals develop certain habits. For example, puppies are often given small treats for doing their business outside during potty training. They learn that if they go in the yard rather than the living room, they will get a tasty kibble. When this training habit is repeated every time for weeks and months, eventually they don't need the kibble and will settle for physical relief and your word of praise.

Similarly, you might have noticed that bad habits also get reinforced, usually unintentionally. Perhaps your pooch is so happy to see you every time you come home that she jumps up on you repeatedly. When it happened at first, you appreciated that your pup was happy to see you and let her jump, maybe even rubbing her ears and talking sweetly. After a dozen or so returns home, though, you don't think her greeting method is so cute, especially when it's applied to everyone and anyone who comes through the door.

Most dog trainers and vets will tell you that both positive and negative habits develop similarly, although you might not notice unless you're paying close attention or have been taught to be intentional. According to veterinarian Sophie Yin, "It turns out that the solution to most behavior problems in pets is equally simple and IF you follow the plan, equally successful. All you need to know is one thing—that animals repeat behaviors that are reinforced."[18]

Whether you've witnessed this training secret in action or not, Dr. Yin explains that the key is being consistent and intentional. "It's just a matter of approaching all problems systematically by thinking about the behavior you'd rather have and how the unwanted behavior was unintentionally reinforced. Once you do this regularly, your understanding and relationship with your pet will be behaviorally rich."[19]

While you're certainly not an animal or anyone's pet, this training secret illustrates the process required to break your own bad habits to adopt other good ones. It's a matter of reinforcement.

- Have you ever tried to train an animal or pet? How would you describe the process?

- Do you agree that the power of reinforcement is the secret to developing both bad habits and good ones? Why or why not?

- When you think about one habit you would like to eliminate, what has been the reinforcing reward or payoff that gives it staying power?

- When you consider a positive habit you've already developed, what reward or reinforcement do you get from doing it?

EXPLORING GOD'S WORD

You may recall from chapter 3.2 in *The Power to Change* that the prophet Daniel was into habits. After the tribes of Israel splintered, the kingdom of Judah, where Daniel lives, is conquered by the Babylonians around 600 BC. Along with his fellow captives, Daniel is transported to Babylon, where he lives out most of his life.

Almost right away, King Nebuchadnezzar identifies a group of Israelites, including Daniel, as potential leaders, and therefore important to influence if not control. The king begins implementing his plan in an obvious, basic way: through the captives' diet. But being forced to eat rich food and drink the king's wine is a dilemma for Daniel. He either refuses and enters a power struggle with his captor—a battle he is sure to lose—or he acquiesces and compromises his faith and culture.

Yet Daniel finds another way, and he uses the power of payoff to do it. Read the passage below, and then answer the questions that follow.

⁵ The king assigned them a daily amount of food and wine from the king's table. They were to be trained for three years, and after that they were to enter the king's service. . . .

⁸ But Daniel resolved not to defile himself with the royal food and wine, and he asked the chief official for permission not to defile himself this way. ⁹ Now God had caused the official to show favor and compassion to Daniel, ¹⁰ but the official told Daniel, "I am afraid of my lord the king, who has assigned your food and drink. Why should he see you looking worse than the other young men your age? The king would then have my head because of you."

¹¹ Daniel then said to the guard whom the chief official had appointed over Daniel, Hananiah, Mishael and Azariah, ¹² "Please test your servants for ten days: Give us nothing but vegetables to eat and water to drink. ¹³ Then compare our appearance with that of the young men who eat the royal food, and treat your servants in accordance with what you see." ¹⁴ So he agreed to this and tested them for ten days.

¹⁵ At the end of the ten days they looked healthier and better nourished than any of the young men who ate the royal food.

DANIEL 1:5, 8–15

- What was the logic Daniel used to convince the guard to allow him and his peers to maintain their diet?

- Why was Daniel willing to trust the ten-day results to prove his point? What was the source of his confidence in his dietary habits?

- How did testing the effectiveness of his preferred diet allow Daniel to avoid a confrontation with the king?

- How does Daniel's example, here and throughout his life, affect your view of personal habits? Why?

EMBRACING THE TRUTH

After Nebuchadnezzar's death, Daniel continued to find favor with the king's royal successors. By the time Darius was king, Daniel had "so distinguished himself among the administrators and the satraps by his exceptional qualities that the king planned to set him over the whole kingdom" (Daniel 6:3). The king's entourage felt jealous and threatened by this, but they couldn't find fault in Daniel's conduct or character. So they set a deadly trap they assumed could not fail.

> [5] *Finally these men said, "We will never find any basis for charges against this man Daniel unless it has something to do with the law of his God."*
>
> [6] *So these administrators and satraps went as a group to the king and said: "May King Darius live forever! [7] The royal administrators, prefects, satraps, advisers and governors have all agreed that the king should issue an edict and enforce the decree that anyone who prays to any god or human being during the next thirty days, except to you, Your Majesty, shall be thrown into the lions' den. [8] Now, Your Majesty, issue the decree and put it in writing so that it cannot be altered—in accordance with the law of the Medes and Persians, which cannot be repealed."*
>
> [9] *So King Darius put the decree in writing.*

[10] *Now when Daniel learned that the decree had been published, he went home to his upstairs room where the windows opened toward Jerusalem. Three times a day he got down on his knees and prayed, giving thanks to his God, just as he had done before.*

DANIEL 6:5–10

- What strikes you most about Daniel's response to the trap his enemies set for him? Why?

- How do you imagine you would respond if you were in Daniel's place? What is one of your default habits when someone threatens or tries to intimidate you?

- Why do you suppose praying, just as he did three times every day, was Daniel's go-to habit in the face of such a life-threatening situation?

- Is prayer and time with God a daily habit you already have in place? If so, how has this habit affected your relationship with him?

CHANGING THE WAY YOU CHANGE

Daniel's habits worked because they were essential parts of the way he lived his life, even in captivity. He didn't need to understand the brain science behind why his habits worked, but you might find a quick review of "the habit loop" helpful to solidify your comprehension.

You'll recall that habits work with the way your brain works. Wired to conserve energy, your brain wants operations to be easy. Which is why your brain loves habits—they allow you to act without thinking. A habit allows good or bad behavior to happen without your brain having to take charge.

Most habits form based on the repetition of a four-step loop:

- The *cue* is a trigger that alerts your brain to go into autopilot by engaging the habit.
- The *craving* is the physical, mental, or emotional need the cue leads you to want to satisfy.
- The *response* is the behavior you routinely fall into.
- The *reward* is how the behavior makes you feel.

Keeping in mind the way habits form can help you assess your approach to breaking bad habits and implementing good ones. Basically, good habits are challenging at first because the pain comes now and your payoff is in the future. Conversely, bad habits are tough to stop because your payoff is more immediate and the pain is in the future.

In exercise 15 at the end of chapter 3.3 in *The Power to Change,* you listed some different cues or triggers, both positive and negative, for some of your habits. Review what you wrote and then answer the following questions.

- Which of the five categories—places, times, moods, moments, and people—had the most positive triggers listed? The most negative?

- What patterns, rhythms, or repeated triggers do you notice from your list?

- Assessing the triggers you listed for all categories, what surprises you the most? Why?

- Using this list to guide you, which negative triggers can be eliminated most easily? Which negative cues will be harder to avoid?

KEEPING THE CHANGE

Starting new healthy habits takes repetition. To get to the point where your brain doesn't have to consciously make a decision and you can just go on autopilot, though, can be tricky. In chapter 3.4 of the book, you explored five qualities that facilitate sticky habits. For any change you desire to make, any habit you want to form, any win you want to achieve, using these five guides—obvious, attractive, easy, communal, repetitious—gives you a better likelihood of success. In exercise 16, you applied and personalized these five guides to habits you want to begin. Review what you wrote and then answer the following questions to help make these five guides even more effective for you.

OBVIOUS

- How would you explain why new habits need to be obvious?

- On a scale of 1 to 10, with 1 being "not so much" and 10 being "super important," how significant do you consider this quality for you in starting new habits? What is the thinking behind your answer?

ATTRACTIVE

- How would you explain why new habits need to be attractive?

- On a scale of 1 to 10, with 1 being "not so much" and 10 being "super important," how significant do you consider this quality for you in starting new habits? What is the thinking behind your answer?

EASY

- How would you explain why new habits need to be easy?

- On a scale of 1 to 10, with 1 being "not so much" and 10 being "super important," how significant do you consider this quality for you in starting new habits? What is the thinking behind your answer?

COMMUNAL

- How would you explain the basis for making new habits communal?

- On a scale of 1 to 10, with 1 being "not so much" and 10 being "super important," how significant do you consider this quality for you in starting new habits? What is the thinking behind your answer?

REPETITIOUS

- How would you explain the reason new habits need to be repetitious?

- On a scale of 1 to 10, with 1 being "not so much" and 10 being "super important," how significant do you consider this quality for you in starting new habits? What is the thinking behind your answer?

SO GOALS AND END GOALS

*As Christ followers, our end goal, our ultimate win, our true mark
of success is becoming more like him.*

CRAIG GROESCHEL

When you shift from a *so* goal to an *end* goal, expect amazing results. Just ask Dallas Jenkins. A director, writer, and producer for both film and television, Jenkins is best known for his work on *The Chosen*, the series he created about the life of Jesus. Financed by more than 16,000 investors who raised more than $11 million by crowdfunding, *The Chosen* portrays stories about Christ, all inspired by accounts in the Bible. Seasons 1 and 2, each with eight episodes, have been well received by critics and viewed by millions around the world.[20]

But Jenkins' goal for *The Chosen* was not to become rich, famous, praised by believers, or known for his multi-hyphenate talents. He told an interviewer, "I got to a place in my career and in my life spiritually, after the failure of my previous movie, which had bombed at the box office, and God really stepped in and got ahold of my heart and my priorities. I got to a place where I genuinely didn't care about the results of anything that I did as long as I truly believed God had called me to it. . . . God had to break me to get me to that place. But once you're there, it's a superpower."[21]

When you focus on using your training and habits to fulfill an end goal, you don't worry about the results. You trust that God will use you according to his purposes and not your own. You're free to fail but perhaps more importantly to succeed beyond anything you can imagine.

- How has your perspective on your big goals changed since starting this study? What has contributed to this shift?

- What are some of the *so* goals—ones focused on your future conditional success—that you've set for yourself?

- How does letting go of your so goals and focusing on end goals shift your definition of success? Why?

- What do you think Dallas Jenkins means when he says that focusing only on what God wants you to do is a superpower? What would having this superpower look like for you?

EXPLORING GOD'S WORD

So goals eventually boomerang their benefits back to you. End goals are focused on what is eternal because they're all about what God wants. Any given goal might even look the same when observed by others, but the results and how you handle them differ greatly. Basically, it all comes down to focus and motivation. Why are you chasing this goal? And for whom are you doing it?

This tension is as old as human nature, going back to Adam and Eve. They had the choice to obey God and do what he wanted them to do or to rebel and focus on what they wanted at the time. And you know how that turned out for them. Jesus addressed this dilemma with his followers, making the consequences of personal choice quite clear:

> [34] *Then, calling the crowd to join his disciples, he said, "If any of you wants to be my follower, you must give up your own way, take up your cross, and follow me. [35] If you try to hang on to your life, you will lose it. But if you give up your life for my*

sake and for the sake of the Good News, you will save it. ³⁶ And what do you benefit if you gain the whole world but lose your own soul? ³⁷ Is anything worth more than your soul? ³⁸ If anyone is ashamed of me and my message in these adulterous and sinful days, the Son of Man will be ashamed of that person when he returns in the glory of his Father with the holy angels."

MARK 8:34–38 NLT

- What has it meant for you to "take up your cross" and follow Jesus? What does taking up your cross look like most days?

- What are some goals you've had in the past that were tethered to your ego? When have you tried to hang on to your own life?

- When have you achieved certain goals only to feel disappointed or even depressed by how little they suddenly meant? What caused your discontentment?

- Think about one or two of the big goals you've set for yourself during this study. What does success look like for each of them?

EMBRACING THE TRUTH

You can usually tell what kind of goals you have by looking at the consequences of your habits and the goals they're trying to fulfill. Again, keep in mind that the habits and goals may appear the same. For example, you may want to eat healthier food and lose fifteen pounds this year. But what is ultimately motivating you? Is it your desire to look good and feel attractive? Or to take care of your body because it's the temple of God's Spirit? The two are not mutually exclusive, but one is always going to outweigh the other.

Another way to tell the difference between a so goal and an end goal is to see how your habits and goals line up with God's Word. Obviously, if they blatantly oppose his commandments and guidelines for believers, you've got a problem. But how do your goals line up with what you know God wants for you? Jesus said you can tell by looking at your foundation.

> [24] *"Therefore everyone who hears these words of mine and puts them into practice is like a wise man who built his house on the rock.* [25] *The rain came down, the streams rose, and the winds blew and beat against that house; yet it did not fall, because it had its foundation on the rock.* [26] *But everyone who hears these words of mine and does not put them into practice is like a foolish man who built his house on sand.* [27] *The rain came down, the streams rose, and the winds blew and beat against that house, and it fell with a great crash."*
>
> MATTHEW 7:24–27

● What does it look like for your goals to be built on rock and not on sand?

● When have you set a goal because you believed God wanted you to do it, but it gradually became motivated by how it benefited you?

● Notice how Jesus uses similar phrasing to contrast each scenario: "everyone who hears these words of mine and puts them into practice is like . . ." and "everyone who hears these words of mine and does not put them into practice is like. . . ." What is the significance of both hearing his words and practicing them?

● Have you ever considered that the reason you've never reached certain goals is because of their focus being only on you? Explain.

CHANGING THE WAY YOU CHANGE

As a follower of Jesus, you want goals that are not about what you get or even what you do, but who you are becoming by pursuing those goals. Not getting, not doing, becoming. Not getting out of debt to buy more stuff to fill the emptiness inside you. Not exercising and losing weight because you think it will finally cause others to love and affirm you the way you want. Not being a better wife so the women in your small group will admire and envy you.

If your goals are to succeed beyond a human, surface, temporary, earthly level, then they require a different focus and motivation. Writing to the Colossians, Paul addresses this shift: "You have been raised to life with Christ. Now set your heart on what is in heaven, where Christ rules at God's right side. Think about what is up there, not about what is here on earth. You died, which means that your life is hidden with Christ, who sits beside God. . . . Each of you is now a new person. You are becoming more and more like your Creator, and you will understand him better" (Colossians 3:1–3, 10 CEV).

In other words, forget about who you *were*. Know who you *are* in Christ and who you want to *become* in him.

How do you do that? Paul continues: "Don't be controlled by your body. Kill every desire for the wrong kind of sex. Don't be immoral or indecent or have evil thoughts. Don't be greedy, which is the same as worshiping idols. . . . You must quit being angry, hateful, and evil. You must no longer say insulting or cruel things about others. And stop lying to each other. You have given up your old way of life with its habits" (verses 5, 8–9 CEV).

If you want to become who God wants you to become, there are some habits you need to give up. Some goals you need to reexamine.

- Which of your current goals and habits needs to be recentered on becoming more like Jesus rather than doing, achieving, or accomplishing?

- How do your priority goals strengthen your relationship with God? How do they make you more like Jesus?

- Looking at Paul's list of what needs to stop, does anything stand out or especially apply to you? Why?

- Fill in the blank: The goal presently coming between me and God most often is

  _____.

KEEPING THE CHANGE

When becoming more like Jesus is the driving force of your life, success is no longer out there somewhere, ahead of you, someday in the future. You can be successful today by taking another step toward Christlikeness. By doing what you know is right. By obeying the call God has placed on your life.

That is the thing about your habits. You may think of them as actions or stepping stones. But they are way more than that. Your habits reveal who you are and who you're becoming.

Spend several minutes in prayer, confessing areas that don't reflect who you are and who God wants you to be. Thank him for the gift of his Son and the example Jesus provides for how to live and grow and know God. Ask him for the strength, power, and wisdom to choose goals that reflect his glory shining through you.

PART 4

SOWING. NOT REAPING.

What you're sowing today will determine the harvest of your future. Your present habits are foreshadowing what your life will look like next year. The life you are living right now is shaping the life you will live tomorrow. You may have the best intentions and the highest hopes, but they won't change you. If you keep doing what you've been doing, you'll keep getting what you've been getting. But if you sow today for your success tomorrow, you will discover that you reap more than you sowed. Here are this section's key principles:

- Successful people do consistently what other people do occasionally.
- You need a power you don't possess.
- Value progress over perfection.
- If you don't like what you're reaping, change what you're sowing. If you don't like the harvest, change the seed.
- You reap more than you sow.
- A small change can change everything.
- You will reap a harvest if you don't give up.

YOU REAP WHAT YOU SOW

The life you're living today is shaping the life you'll live tomorrow.

CRAIG GROESCHEL

If you have an entrepreneurial spirit, then you can appreciate a thirteen-year-old who viewed his job delivering newspapers (remember those?) as a business. Apparently, he also talked to trainers at the horse track and eavesdropped on their public conversations with the goal of creating a tip sheet he could sell each week. By high school, this kid and a buddy purchased a used pinball machine for twenty-five bucks, which they installed in their local barbershop. They used profits from that venture to buy and install more pinball machines. By the time they established three lucrative locations, they sold their fledgling business for $1,200.[22]

Those early experiences foretold the business and financial acumen of one of the world's most renowned investors, Warren Buffett. As the longtime chairman and CEO of the investment company Berkshire Hathaway, Buffett has accumulated a net worth estimated at over $100 billion.[23] He credits much of his success to his singular focus.[24]

Buffett doesn't check social media or write emails.[25] He's not a collector of expensive items—art, cars, houses, watches—that broadcast his wealth.[26] By many standards, Buffett lives a modest life. But his passion for business, for investing, for studying stocks, bonds, and financial markets started early in his life and has never wavered. He became successful by doing what he loves and practicing the habits supporting his passion.

Warren Buffett's life illustrates an essential lesson for lasting change: small seeds planted consistently over time yield a consistent harvest.

- Who is someone exceptionally successful in his or her field or expertise that you admire? Why do you find that person intriguing?

- What do you believe is responsible for this person's success? What has catapulted him or her above so many others who do what that person does?

- Which contributes to a person's success more: their talent or their habits? Why?

- What is presently preventing you from succeeding at the same level as those you admire? How can you pursue their kind of success?

EXPLORING GOD'S WORD

The fanatical consistency of successful people isn't the most important evidence for the fact that your habits shape your life. Nor is the common saying "you reap what you sow" just a clichéd figure of speech. The fundamental law of sowing and reaping is explained most authoritatively in God's Word. Drawing on a basic agrarian metaphor his audience could easily understand, Paul applied the principle of sowing and harvesting in a letter to the Galatians:

> [7] *Do not be deceived: God cannot be mocked. A man reaps what he sows.* [8] *Whoever sows to please their flesh, from the flesh will reap destruction; whoever sows to please the Spirit, from the Spirit will reap eternal life.* [9] *Let us not become weary in doing good, for at the proper time we will reap a harvest if we do not give up.*

> **GALATIANS 6:7–9**

Notice how Paul begins his explanation—"Do not be deceived"—emphasizing the importance of seeing clearly and believing what is true. And what is true is the reality of getting out what you put in. Spiritually speaking, this means if you plant seeds for living sinfully, then you will reap destruction. On the other hand, if you sow to God's Spirit, allowing him to empower and guide you, then your harvest will be an abiding relationship with God for all eternity.

This principle extends beyond agriculture and your spiritual life—it reflects a basic truth about causes and consequences. You will reap what you sow. The results of your life will be based on the daily decisions you make, the regular habits you practice as well as the ones you choose not to practice. You will harvest what you plant.

- How does your life presently reflect your choices and habits from a year ago? From ten years ago?

- What are some ways you have invested in your relationship with God by sowing to the Spirit? What results or spiritual fruit have you experienced?

- What are some ways you have invested in your flesh by sowing sinful choices? What consequences have you faced because of them?

● Why is it essential not to "become weary in doing good"? How is the principle of sowing and reaping a lifelong practice?

EMBRACING THE TRUTH

A bit earlier in Paul's same later to the Galatians, he contrasts bad fruit and good fruit and gives specific examples of each:

> [19] When you follow the desires of your sinful nature, the results are very clear: sexual immorality, impurity, lustful pleasures, [20] idolatry, sorcery, hostility, quarreling, jealousy, outbursts of anger, selfish ambition, dissension, division, [21] envy, drunkenness, wild parties, and other sins like these. Let me tell you again, as I have before, that anyone living that sort of life will not inherit the Kingdom of God.
> [22] But the Holy Spirit produces this kind of fruit in our lives: love, joy, peace, patience, kindness, goodness, faithfulness, [23] gentleness, and self-control. There is no law against these things!
>
> GALATIANS 5:19–23 NLT

Notice the seeds causing certain kinds of crops here. When you follow your own sinful desires without regard for God, his laws, and your relationship with him, then here's what you get: a garden full of garbage. When you seek God and yield to the work of his Holy Spirit in your life, you can expect a bumper crop of blessings. You plant that way; you harvest that way. You sow this way; you reap this way.

When you put a certain type of seed in the ground, you get a harvest that corresponds with the seed you planted. If you plant bad habits, don't be deceived and expect good outcomes. If you plant good habits, you'll get good outcomes. This holds true in agriculture and in life. Every single time without exceptions. You reap what you sow.

- If most people want better fruit in their lives, why do they fail to change what they've been planting? What seeds do you need to change to yield better fruit?

- What is the ultimate harvest of sowing a life based on selfish, sinful choices? What is the ultimate harvest of sowing a life based on spiritual, godly choices?

- Which habits continue to be pesky weeds in your spiritual garden? When do they tend to spring up?

- Which habits fertilize and nourish the seeds in your spiritual garden? Which areas need more spiritual fertilizer right now?

CHANGING THE WAY YOU CHANGE

In order to reap the harvest you want and reach the goals you know God has called you to pursue, you must commit to persevering for the long haul. And perhaps the most important way you commit is by being consistent, doing the small habits and making the mundane choices that gradually and cumulatively yield significant harvests.

For this reason, focus on sowing more than reaping. If you really want to replace your *so* goals with *end* goals, then be consistent with planting the seeds God has given you. Don't look ahead and wonder what your harvest will look like or how much you'll reap. Just sow. Just do the next thing, keeping the right habits and dropping the bad habits.

Sometimes the challenge with sowing small consistent habits is impatience and perceived lack of results. You may even be at this point right now in practicing what you've been learning in this workbook. You began by defining your win. You broke it down into habits you can practice daily. You made some progress and feel good about it. But then you realize you still have such a long way to go.

In these moments, you must stop the negative chatter in your mind urging you to give up. Stop looking ahead at the huge fields of the future that only have tiny sprouts right now. You must keep going. Because what you're pursuing is bigger than you and way too important.

- What are some habits you may have overlooked as too small or insignificant that can nonetheless help you reach a goal?

- What significant or crucial habit is not taking hold the way you want it to? What do you believe is preventing it from taking root in your life?

- When was the last time you felt discouraged because your goal seemed out of reach? How did you handle your discouragement?

- What is one way you can handle those times when you feel like giving up? What can remind you of the importance of what you're doing?

KEEPING THE CHANGE

Just as farmers water and fertilize their crops to ensure their growth, you can persevere during times of personal drought by looking for little ways to support and nourish your habits.

You may recall how Nehemiah handled the overwhelming task of rebuilding the city walls around Jerusalem. He began by expressing how he felt and prayed before God (see Nehemiah 1:4). Prayer is always a great way to support your habits. Nehemiah knew he couldn't rebuild the wall alone, so he made a plan and delegated tasks, making it a communal effort. Regardless of your goal and habits, enlisting the help of others for support is another vital way to keep persevering.

In addition to prayer and support from others, you can strategize on ways to keep your momentum. You can look ahead and be proactive about avoiding or removing obstacles that have hindered you in the past. You can find ways to make persevering easier.

For example, when your schedule gets full, you might be tempted to quit going to the gym. But instead of letting other demands consume your workout time, you can schedule in your time to exercise like the important appointment it is. Or perhaps you want to make tithing a priority but always struggle when your paycheck gets stretched too thin. If you set up an automatic withdrawal from your account to the place your tithe goes, you wouldn't have to think about it because you've made the decision already.

Now it's your turn. Use the prompts below to help you persevere as you sow the habits that will reap the goals you want most.

• One goal that continues to seem too big for me is _____.

• The habits I'm practicing to pursue this goal include:

- I tend to get discouraged and think about quitting my habits when _____ _____ happens or when my day includes _____ _____.

- Some ways I can water and nourish the seed-habits I'm planting during tough times are:

YOU REAP MORE THAN YOU SOW

A small difference each day adds up and multiplies over time.

CRAIG GROESCHEL

People have been eating wheat in a variety of forms for thousands of years. While most aspects of twenty-first-century wheat farming have changed due to technology, genetic modification, climate concern, risk management, and food equity, the basics of sowing and reaping remain the same. Consequently, growing wheat is not exclusive to huge farms with hundreds of acres and an arsenal of heavy-duty equipment. More people are growing their own wheat in their home gardens and shared allotments.

Whether as a hobby, for health reasons, or to ensure sustainability, these individual gardeners quickly discover that planting wheat yields so much more than expected. It only takes planting one pound of wheat seed to produce about ninety pounds of grain! Or considered another way, you only need around five square feet to produce one cup of flour, the result of grinding and sifting about half a cup of grain.[27]

How can wheat seeds produce such an overabundant crop? Simply put, they grow and multiply. Each wheat kernel planted will eventually produce a stalk with three heads of grain. Each head may contain between fifteen to thirty-five kernels, which means one kernel of wheat can potentially produce more than one hundred more kernels.[28]

Wheat isn't the only seed that can yield much more than the amount planted. The habits you're planting now have the potential to produce a greater impact than you can imagine. You won't just get back what you put in. You will reap so much more than you sowed.

* What surprises you or stands out in the way wheat seeds yield such enormous harvests?

* When have you witnessed something organic (such as a plant or animal) growing bigger than you expected? To what did you attribute the extra growth?

* What is one habit you've maintained for a long time that has snowballed with its positive impact? What have been its benefits?

● What is one habit that you've quit doing that ended up causing a larger negative effect than expected?

EXPLORING GOD'S WORD

When you submit to and obey God, it may seem like a one-time decision. But it's not. You are training yourself to be faithful. You are becoming more like Christ. That one act of obedience proves you trustworthy, trains you in faithfulness, and softens your heart to continue to say yes to God. In other words, you're reaping more than you sowed.

Repeated obedience and submission have a cumulative effective on your faith. They draw you closer to him and allow you to experience the full abundance of living out your God-given purpose. Each act, choice, or habit keeps you tender-hearted and sowing to please the Spirit rather than becoming callous and stony because you were sowing to your flesh. As you read the passages below, notice the cause and effect being described.

> [19] *"I will give them an undivided heart and put a new spirit in them; I will remove from them their heart of stone and give them a heart of flesh.* [20] *Then they will follow my decrees and be careful to keep my laws. They will be my people, and I will be their God.* [21] *But as for those whose hearts are devoted to their vile images and detestable idols, I will bring down on their own heads what they have done, declares the Sovereign LORD."*
>
> EZEKIEL 11:19–21

> [26] *"I will give you a new heart and put a new spirit in you; I will remove from you your heart of stone and give you a heart of flesh.* [27] *And I will put my Spirit in you and move you to follow my decrees and be careful to keep my laws."*
>
> EZEKIEL 36:26–27

- According to these passages, what is the basis or source of an undivided heart and new spirit?

- How does worshipping idols—basically anything other than God—harm or destroy your spiritual fruit?

- What are some of God's decrees and laws that are challenging for you to keep? How have you handled this struggle?

- What long-term, cumulative impact will your spiritual habits have in your relationship with God? With other people?

EMBRACING THE TRUTH

When you're tempted to skip time alone with God or to choose something you know will harm your spirit, you're setting up a ripple effect. Making a wise decision or doing something for God today may feel insignificant or unrelated to other areas of your life. But you have no idea the significance it could grow to have in the future. Remember, what you're doing now determines who you will be years from now.

The inverse is also true. When you don't engage in an essential spiritual habit, such as prayer or reading your Bible or serving others, or when you choose to sin, even if you think of it as an isolated incident, it's not. God's Word says that one little choice can "give the devil a foothold" (Ephesians 4:27) to enter and work in your life. In fact, one little act of disobedience, one little sin, can "harden your heart" and has a way of "turning you away from the living God" (Hebrews 3:8, 12 NLT).

* How does connecting with God every day keep you grounded for that day? For your lifetime?

* What assumptions are you making when you choose to think that what you do or don't do today won't matter in the future?

* When have you given the devil an opportunity to tempt or derail you because of one choice you made? What were the long-term consequences of that choice?

- When have you seen multiple benefits occur from one single act of service, kindness, or compassion?

CHANGING THE WAY YOU CHANGE

You may occasionally find yourself stuck in the tension between *believing* what you do today always matters while also *feeling* like it doesn't make a difference or have a big enough impact. That is when it helps to remember that what you reap will always be more than you sow, even when you can't see it or understand it—perhaps especially then. And in order to focus on your extra impactful harvest, you should also remember the two qualities that give it this more-than-expected turbocharge: the cumulative effect and the compound effect.

You may find the cumulative effect easier to grasp immediately. It's not difficult to acknowledge the way certain things accrete over time to cause an end result that is far bigger than the small steps along the way. And it cuts both ways. When you're sowing good habits and focusing on the goals that God has given you, then there's a snowball effect that can turn into an avalanche. One decision, action, or word can set in motion consequences far greater than you can foresee.

On the other hand, the cumulative effect can become a kind of erosion that chips away at something you once thought solid and secure—your faith, your marriage, your relationship with your kids. When bad choices pile up, they carve away at the habits and goals you most want to practice and attain.

The compound effect may seem trickier to grasp. As you read in chapter 4.4 in *The Power to Change*, the best example of the compound effect probably comes from the way compound interest works when you're saving money. When you keep sowing and investing from what you reap, you keep reaping more and more. Think of the compound effect as a kind of contagious result. It often happens when you begin to see one change in your life and feel motivated to continue on in order to see even more.

Together, the cumulative and compound effects remind you that everything adds up and can grow bigger over time.

- When have you seen the cumulative effect occur because of a habit you were diligent to practice?

- When have you seen the cumulative effect hurt you because of a habit you let slide?

- When you experience results greater than you expected, what are your expectations from then on? Do you want to rush to the end of the compound effect? Explain.

- Which effect motivates you to pay attention to "the small stuff" more closely? Why?

KEEPING THE CHANGE

You've likely benefited from a single kind act, spoken word, or small gift received from another person. These often occur just when you need encouragement most and can make the difference in your attitude and choices for the rest of the day. The person who gifted you may have no idea how much your interaction with them meant for you. Sometimes the best serendipitous gifts of this kind come from strangers, people who don't know us and therefore don't expect anything in return.

Now it's time to give back, help out, and pay it forward. For an entire day, look for as many opportunities as possible to bless others. Pay sincere compliments to coworkers, hand a large bill over to the homeless person on the corner, buy lunch for the next table without its diners knowing, take out the trash without being prompted, cook dinner for your spouse. If it helps, imagine that your job for that day is to be God's ambassador to everyone around you.

At the end of your day (or the next morning), spend some time in prayer reflecting on your experience. Consider when and who God might be calling you to bless next. Think about any habits you might want to add or subtract.

YOU REAP AFTER YOU SOW

You won't see the results you want today. Be patient.
You've planted the right seeds. The harvest will come.

CRAIG GROESCHEL

In 1952, *Collier's* magazine published a sci-fi story by Ray Bradbury titled "A Sound of Thunder." Bradbury went on to write numerous stories, novels, films, and screenplays, including perhaps his best-known, *Fahrenheit 451*. But in this particular short story, he introduced an idea that continues to reverberate in quantum physics, popular culture, and beyond.

Known as the "butterfly effect," the concept comes from the end of Bradbury's story, when a time-traveling hunter named Eckels, after going back millions of years to kill a T. Rex, returns to his own time period in 2055 and discovers significant changes. Trying to determine the catalyst that altered time and history, Eckels notices a crushed butterfly on his boot.[29]

While Bradbury's story may have been the basis of the concept, the term "butterfly effect" is said to have originated in the 1960s with a meteorologist named Edward Lorenz. He described how the beating of a butterfly's wings in one part of the world could eventually cause a storm in another place thousands of miles away. His intention was "to illustrate chaos theory and the impossibility of predicting the weather more than a few days or weeks in advance."[30]

Today, the term has been mainstreamed and appropriated in various fields and genres. Sci-fi and fantasy movies and TV series rely on the butterfly effect as a plot staple. Physicists still use it to describe the way even one small variation can have dramatic consequences. But the concept is also appropriate for illustrating the power of habits for change: one small, seemingly insignificant habit could cause a life-changing difference in your future.

- Have you heard of the butterfly effect before? When and in what context?

- Do you agree with the basic premise that something as slight as a butterfly flapping its wings could result in major consequences? Why or why not?

- What is one small gesture, action, or seemingly random event you believe has changed the course of your life? What difference has it made?

- What is one new habit you've recently implemented? Looking ahead, what difference would continuing with this habit ten years into the future have on your life?

EXPLORING GOD'S WORD

In part 3, you contrasted the effectiveness of *hoping* for change versus taking action and creating a *habit* for change. This kind of hope may have seemed like magic thinking, a wistful wish for your future apparently detached from your ability to do anything about it. Hope in this regard is indeed powerless to help you make and sustain changes in your life.

There's another kind of hope, though—the kind described in the Bible. Hope in this sense is inherent to your faith. This is hope founded not on daydreams or your imagination, but on the reality of Jesus Christ. In his letter to the Romans, Paul describes this hope as the result of knowing and practicing other habits:

> [1] *Therefore, since we have been justified through faith, we have peace with God through our Lord Jesus Christ,* [2] *through whom we have gained access by faith into this grace in which we now stand. And we boast in the hope of the glory of God.* [3] *Not only so, but we also glory in our sufferings, because we know that suffering produces perseverance;* [4] *perseverance, character; and character, hope.* [5] *And hope does not put us to shame, because God's love has been poured out into our hearts through the Holy Spirit, who has been given to us.*
>
> **ROMANS 5:1–5**

- How would you explain the difference between the kind of hope discussed previously and the kind of hope Paul's talking about here?

- Based on this passage, why should you glory in your suffering? What good does suffering do?

- How have you experienced suffering that produces perseverance? What effect does persevering through hard times have on your character?

- What does it mean to have a character that rests on hope? When have you experienced this kind of hope?

EMBRACING THE TRUTH

Sustaining hope, the kind your faith is built upon, is rarely easy—especially when you're focused on making changes in your life. On the frontline of a challenging day, it's tempting to believe your small decisions and consistent efforts don't matter. That there's nothing you can do to change things.

When you're struggling in your marriage, when your body can't seem to heal, when your finances leave you reeling, when you're praying for a loved one battling addiction, it's hard to hope for something better. You find yourself thinking, "It's bad, hopeless, and it will never get better no matter what I do or don't do." You're weary of trying to make things better. You've tried and tried, but nothing good seems to last for long. You wonder where God is and what he's up to with your circumstances.

This is the time to take a breath and get out of your head and into your heart. This is when you dig in and refuse to quit doing what you've committed to doing. This is when you trust God and denounce the enemy's lies. This is when you must remember there's so much more going on than you can see and understand with your human limitations.

> [16] *Therefore we do not lose heart. Though outwardly we are wasting away, yet inwardly we are being renewed day by day.* [17] *For our light and momentary troubles are achieving for us an eternal glory that far outweighs them all.* [18] *So we fix our eyes not on what is seen, but on what is unseen, since what is seen is temporary, but what is unseen is eternal.*
>
> 2 CORINTHIANS 4:16–18

- How would you elaborate on the contrast between what is going on outwardly versus inwardly? Why is it important to recognize this contrast?

- When have you been most tempted to quit trying to do what you know God has called you to do? What factors contributed to this temptation?

- How can you practice fixing your eyes on what is unseen? How can you stay focused on what is eternal?

- What encourages you not to lose heart when you're having a tough day? What reminds you of what is true and not what *appears* true?

CHANGING THE WAY YOU CHANGE

When you reach your breaking point, remember that there's a breakthrough up ahead of you. If you're on a plateau where nothing seems to be improving, remember that being consistent makes a crucial difference. Even though you can't see progress now, just the fact that you're persevering means you're winning.

During those times when you feel stuck, sometimes it's helpful to do a reality check and look more carefully at where you are. Your expectations may be so high or perfectionistic that you're unable to see the tiny, incremental progress you've been making. You can slip into an all-or-nothing perspective without even realizing it.

Sometimes just putting on your running shoes and going around the block is a win even if you didn't run the three miles you were supposed to run. But why were you "supposed to"? Keep a tight rein on those "supposed tos" and "shoulds" because you often pressure yourself beyond what is feasible, necessary, or realistic. Focus on *small* and *consistent* in order to invest in your future success.

- Do you tend to push yourself to do and be a certain way in order to feel good about yourself? Or are you more prone to take a laid-back approach and try not to notice when you let things slide? Explain your response.

- Think back to when you started this workbook. What were your expectations about how you would change? Knowing what you know now, how have your expectations changed?

- When was the last time you couldn't complete a habit the way you wanted? What was your response—to skip it altogether or to improvise and do what you could?

- Which habits or practices could benefit from lowered expectations? Which might improve if you expected more from yourself?

KEEPING THE CHANGE

In order to experience the long-range benefits that will come from your future harvest, you must keep sowing right now. It's not easy. It's not convenient. It doesn't feel good much of the time. But refusing to give up is a habit in itself that will sustain you and help you persevere.

It seems fitting that the butterfly effect refers to a small change having a big consequence because of the metamorphosis required to produce a butterfly. Starting out as an earthbound caterpillar, these beautiful creatures emerge from their chrysalis and take flight. As corny as it might sound, you're doing the same thing—being transformed by the small choices you make every day.

PART 5

GOD'S POWER.
NOT WILLPOWER.

No matter how well-planned, intentioned, or practiced, you cannot consistently do the right things you want to do in your own power. Left to rely on your own resources and willpower, you will eventually get discouraged and quit. You simply don't possess what you need to succeed on your own. Fortunately, though, you never have to feel defeated because God has the power that you lack. You can't, but God can. And he will, if you turn to his power. Here are this final section's main points:

- You think you can, but you can't.
- You can't, but God can.
- And God will, if you turn to his power.
- Willpower doesn't work, but God's power does—it's available, accessible, active, and abundant.
- If you renew and remain before the moment, if you acknowledge and ask in the moment, you will have God's power to walk by the Spirit.
- When you're winning, you're winning. When you're losing, you're learning.

YOU CAN'T, BUT GOD CAN

We stay stuck because we rely on willpower instead of God's power.

CRAIG GROESCHEL

B eing stuck is no fun. If you're claustrophobic, being stuck on an elevator might be your worst nightmare. Nicholas White knows firsthand how it feels. Back in 1999 White, a thirty-four-year-old production manager for Business Week in New York City, was working late one Friday night when he wanted a smoke. From the forty-third floor of the McGraw Hill Building, White descended to the lobby, had his cigarette, and returned for the ride back up. Only his ascending ride stopped after a few seconds—and ended up not starting again for forty-one hours.[31]

Nicholas White wasn't discovered and rescued until late Sunday afternoon. By then, he had gone through the gamut of emotions during his traumatic ordeal. In 2008 White's story anchored a lengthy piece on elevators in *The New Yorker*, "Up and Then Down," by Nick Paumgarten. Tracing White's journey following his elevator entrapment, Paumgarten discovered how White's life fell apart—he sued his employer but didn't settle out of court until four years later. In the meantime, he lost his job, his friends and colleagues at work, and most of his life as he had known it before that fateful Friday night.[32]

Paumgarten concludes, "Looking back on the experience now, with a peculiarly melancholic kind of bewilderment, he [White] recognizes that he walked onto an elevator one night, with his life in one kind of shape, and emerged from it with his life in another. Still, he now sees that it wasn't so much the elevator that changed him as his reaction to it."[33]

You don't have to get trapped in an elevator to feel stuck. And how you react to being stuck is indeed the key to moving forward again.

- What is one particular fear you have? What kinds of situations cause you the most anxiety?

- When was the last time you felt stuck because of your mood, mindset, or circumstances? What would you compare it to?

- What is your reaction when you realize you're stuck where you are, either literally or figuratively? Do you tend to take action and will yourself forward or just wait it out?

- When have you hit a wall or plateaued in your progress with the habits you've been practicing? What keeps you going?

EXPLORING GOD'S WORD

If you've ever tried to change, then you know how it feels to get stuck. You try to keep going, doing what you want to do. You make progress, then slide back to where you started. So you try harder. But the back-and-forth cycle keeps you stuck in place, which can begin to feel like you're farther behind than when you started.

No matter how strong you are, no matter how exceptional your character and fortitude and grit, you cannot change in your own power. Because ultimately, willpower does not work. You think it can, and it can sustain you for a while, but eventually you run out—out of energy, out of focus, out of power.

When your willpower runs out, you begin to feel weak, powerless, even helpless. You start to feel numb and detached from caring about whether you change or not. You feel shame for not being strong enough, for not being able to change in your own power. You're not alone in this downward spiral. The apostle Paul experienced this kind of downward slide until he realized that he was in the perfect position to rely on God's power.

7 Therefore, in order to keep me from becoming conceited, I was given a thorn in my flesh, a messenger of Satan, to torment me. 8 Three times I pleaded with the Lord to take it away from me. 9 But he said to me, "My grace is sufficient for you, for my power is made perfect in weakness." Therefore I will boast all the more gladly about my weaknesses, so that Christ's power may rest on me. 10 That is why, for Christ's sake, I delight in weaknesses, in insults, in hardships, in persecutions, in difficulties. For when I am weak, then I am strong.

2 CORINTHIANS 12:7–10

- Can you identify with Paul's "thorn" in the flesh? What persistent bad habit has continued to cause you pain, discomfort, and discouragement?

- How does being dependent on God's grace and strength empower you to do what your willpower simply can't do?

- How is God's power made perfect by the weaknesses of willpower in your life? How have your struggles caused you to recognize you can't do it alone?

- Why is recognizing your weaknesses and struggles cause for "delight"? How can depending on God's power get you unstuck?

EMBRACING THE TRUTH

As you've experienced before, willpower can only get you so far. A burst of willpower fueled by stubborn determination gives you a little success, but it never lasts. Willpower is like a muscle, and muscles get fatigued to the point that they have very little strength. Once your willpower is tired and depleted, you find you're back to your old, disappointing, unable-to-change self.

Your failure can overwhelm you with guilt, which only reinforces your negative self-talk. Instead of focusing on particular instances of failure and seeing what you can learn from them, you conclude that you're the problem. Because you can't change on your own, you must be deficient, inadequate, weak, and bad. Beat yourself up enough, and you don't want to get up and try again. You resign yourself to being stuck indefinitely.

Once again, Paul knew all about this cycle of trying, failing, hoping, and failing again. He describes the crazy back-and-forth, two-steps-forward-one-step-back sensation in Romans 7. After riding this internal roller coaster, Paul concludes with what we've all felt during those times when we're stuck: "Oh, what a miserable person I am! Who will free me from this life that is dominated by sin and death?" (Romans 7:24 NLT). But he immediately knows the answer, and so do you—"Thank God! The answer is in Jesus Christ our Lord" (verse 25 NLT).

- Do you consider yourself a strong-willed person? Why or why not?

- Regardless of how strong you believe your willpower to be, when have you experienced it running out of steam lately? How did you respond?

- What are the negative, self-critical labels you default to when you feel like you've failed in your struggle? When do you feel like a "miserable person"?

- How does knowing the solution to your power shortage give you spiritual hope to continue? How does the power of Christ get you unstuck?

CHANGING THE WAY YOU CHANGE

In chapter 5.1 of *The Power to Change*, there's a modern update of Paul's shame-cycle rant in Romans 7. Review it along with Romans 7:15-24 in your favorite version of the Bible. Now it's your turn to personalize this passage and insert your own specific struggles. You can certainly have some fun with this, but also take it seriously. Be as honest as you can, knowing that no one else needs to see this but you. Use the prompts below to assist you in composing your personal update.

I don't really understand myself, because I want to do what is right, especially _____

_____ *.*

But that is not what I do! Instead I do _____

_____ *, which I hate!*

I know I'm the one doing wrong, compelled by the sin living in me, which explains why I feel stuck, like _____ *.*

I want to do the right thing so often, I even try to _____

_____ *, but I can't—not for long. Realizing how stuck I am, wanting to change but unable to do it in my own power, leaves me feeling* _____ *about myself.*

My life seems bound by the tension of being stuck this way. I want to do what is right but inevitably do what is wrong. I love God with all my heart, but still I do things like _____*,* _____ *, and* _____ *.*

There's this sinful pull at war with my mind, making me feel like I'm _____

_____ *in my ability to change.*

Oh, what a _____ *person I am! Who can break this cycle that I'm stuck in?*

ROMANS 7:15–24 (ACCORDING TO YOU)

KEEPING THE CHANGE

While God is well aware of the struggle you've been having, pour your heart out before him and share what it's been like for you to try so hard and yet see so little progress. Let him know that you love him and want to do all that he has called you to do. Use this passage from James as a model for humbling yourself before the Lord. The prayer starter below can help, but definitely make the prayer your own.

[7] So humble yourselves before God. Resist the devil, and he will flee from you. [8] Come close to God, and God will come close to you. Wash your hands, you sinners; purify your hearts, for your loyalty is divided between God and the world. [9] Let there be tears for what you have done. Let there be sorrow and deep grief. Let there be sadness instead of laughter, and gloom instead of joy. [10] Humble yourselves before the Lord, and he will lift you up in honor.

JAMES 4:7-10 NLT

Dear God, I get so frustrated with myself. You know what has happened with all my previous attempts to change. I always try harder and forget that only your power can fuel my hopes and habits for the long run. Forgive me, Lord, for trying to push my way forward on will-power alone. Give me your strength and stamina, through the power of your Holy Spirit in me, so that I can keep going, permanently and eternally unstuck as I experience the lasting changes conforming me to the image of your Son, Jesus. I pray this in his name. Amen.

RENEW, REMAIN, ASK, ACKNOWLEDGE

Move forward in confidence, knowing God gives generously and will provide all the power you need and more.

CRAIG GROESCHEL

People battling addiction often realize they can only win their battle by relying on God's power. Such is the case for Ryan Longmuir, now an award-winning caterer and successful businessman in his native Scotland, who has lived drug free for more than two decades. Ryan grew up in the small Scottish town of Cumbernauld, where he and his friends began experimenting with drugs when he was twelve.[34]

"I tried everything—cocaine, Valium, ecstasy, speed, heroin. . . . I'd go on benders for two or three days at a time, and take five or ten ecstasy tablets in one night," Longmuir revealed in an interview with the BBC. "From the age of fifteen to twenty I took drugs every single day."[35]

His deep dependence on drugs came to a halt, however, after Ryan was arrested at twenty. In addition to taking drugs every day, he had also been dealing them. Facing a possible jail sentence, he phoned a friend who said she would pray for him and encouraged him to pray as well. Ryan admits he thought she was "off her head" but was just desperate enough to try it. "I got down beside my bed and I said, 'I don't believe that there is a God, but if you're real then show me that you're real and I'll believe in you.' "[36]

The turning point came shortly afterward when he met two women hitchhiking. They took him to lunch and then to their church, even inviting him to stay with them while he sorted out his next steps. Their kindness became a catalyst for Ryan's commitment to God and the resulting freedom from his addiction. Ryan found that he quickly embraced his faith and experienced an immediate change. His desire for drugs disappeared, he threw his remaining stash into the sea, and he has been clean ever since then.

Knowing that his life could easily have turned out quite differently, Ryan does his best to help others battling addiction and often employs ex-offenders and those in recovery. Ryan's life is a testimony to the power of God to transform a person's life from the inside out.

- Ryan's testimony includes immediate freedom from his addiction. Have you known someone who experienced the same kind of instant transformation? Who was the person and what was the situation?

- Many times, the kind of freedom Ryan experienced doesn't happen right away. What destructive habit have you been battling for a long time?

● How has the power of God already changed your life?

● What are some of the turning points or milestones in your faith journey when you have surrendered yourself to God?

EXPLORING GOD'S WORD

To sustain lasting change in your life, you're well aware that willpower won't cut it. Whoever you want to become or whoever you want to stop being, you will never do it alone. Whatever it is that you want to do or stop doing, you need more than you can muster. You need the limitless, supernatural power of God.

God can empower you to do what you can't do on your own. Through his power, you can do the hard things and win life's battles. He can help you keep loving someone who is difficult to love. God can shift your attitude to serve others when you used to prefer being served. He can help you take risks and step out in faith. But you have to be willing to tap into God's power in the moment when you need him most.

Perhaps Jesus sums it up best: "I am the vine; you are the branches. If you remain in me and I in you, you will bear much fruit; apart from me you can do nothing" (John 15:5). Just as tendrils rely on vines for the sustenance to grow, you rely on Christ as the power source for your life. With him, you bear much fruit. Without him, you can do nothing. Similarly, Paul instructs you to walk in the Spirit, allowing God's power to pull you away from gratifying yourself with what is pleasurable, easy, or immediately fulfilling.

16 So I say, walk by the Spirit, and you will not gratify the desires of the flesh. 17 For the flesh desires what is contrary to the Spirit, and the Spirit what is contrary to the flesh. They are in conflict with each other, so that you are not to do whatever you want. 18 But if you are led by the Spirit, you are not under the law.

GALATIANS 5:16–18

- How does your life look different now than before you started relying on Christ and walking by the Spirit? What is the greatest change or difference?

- What struggle or stubborn habit seems to have remained constant even after you began following Jesus? What payoff or temporary reward does this habit provide for you?

- In order to abide in Jesus and walk by the Spirit, which of your present priorities needs readjusting? Why?

- How does walking in the Spirit by faith change your perspective on your struggles?

EMBRACING THE TRUTH

In those crucial moments when you're tempted to surf online again, to buy more jewelry, to worry again, to cheat again, to gossip again, to drink again, or to call your ex again, how do you rely on God's power—rather than willpower—to overcome the temptation to do wrong? How do you walk in the Spirit in those moments? Here are four strategies, two for practicing before temptation comes and two for using when you're in the middle of it:

- *Renew* your mind.
- *Remain* in Jesus as your home.
- *Ask* God directly for his help.
- *Acknowledge* your need.

Here's a quick review for easy reference.

RENEW

To walk in the Spirit, in God's power, you need to renew your mind: "Do not conform to the pattern of this world, but be transformed by the renewing of your mind. Then you will be able to test and approve what God's will is—his good, pleasing and perfect will" (Romans 12:2).

As a follower of Jesus, you're called to live in a way that is holy and pleasing to God. He invites you to be changed, to be different from the rest of the world. The key to living out God's "good, pleasing and perfect will" is being "transformed by the renewing of your mind."

When you allow God to change the way you think, it will change how you act, how you respond to opportunities and temptations, how you treat other people. Renewing your mind will change everything.

REMAIN

To walk in the Spirit, you need to remain anchored in your relationship with Christ. "Remain in me, and I will remain in you. For a branch cannot produce fruit if it is severed from the vine, and you cannot be fruitful unless you remain in me. Yes, I am the vine; you are the branches. Those who remain in me, and I in them, will produce much fruit. For apart from me you can do nothing" (John 15:4–5 NLT).

He tells you, "Remain in me." When you do, God's power will be unleashed in your life. You will be fruitful. You'll be able to live the life that God created you to live.

ASK

When you're being tempted, instead of giving up and giving in, you can look up and ask God for power to resist. When you look up in prayer, you connect to the God who loves you, has what you need, and is just waiting for you to ask. He is your Abba Father and loves helping you to be more like his Son.

James describes those "desires that battle within you" (4:1). The reason you sometimes lose the battle stems from failing to ask for what you need: "You do not have because you do not ask God" (4:2). So ask. James makes it emphatically clear: "You should ask God, who gives generously to all without finding fault, and it will be given to you" (1:5).

God wants to give you his power, and in the moment of temptation, his power is what you need.

ACKNOWLEDGE

Acknowledging "I can't" is the path to possessing a power you don't possess. What you need is the God of resurrection working on your behalf, strengthening you, his power coursing through your mind, heart, and body, releasing you from what has held you back for so long.

When you doubt yourself—and you will—ignore that voice and acknowledge that you don't have the power you need. Admit, with Paul, "I want to do what is right, but I can't" (Romans 7:18 nlt), reminding yourself that "apart from [Jesus] you can do nothing" (John 15:5).

CHANGING THE WAY YOU CHANGE

To personalize and strategize how each of these four can benefit you most, answer the following questions:

- Which one of these four—renew, remain, ask, acknowledge—is the hardest for you to remember and practice? What is challenging about it?

- Which one of these four are you already practicing in order to receive God's power? When was the last time you used it to strengthen your faith-based power?

- What is one of the best ways for you to renew your mind? How does it help you remain in Jesus as your power source?

- How often do you directly ask God for the help you need when you need it? What causes you to overlook or ignore asking for what he wants to give you?

KEEPING THE CHANGE

Out of all the verses included in part 5 of *The Power to Change*, some likely resonate with you now more than others. Go back through the chapters in part 5 and make a short list of the verses or passages that strike you as especially important for your success moving forward. Make a brief note next to each one indicating why it's meaningful to you. Text your list to yourself and maybe even print a copy—whatever helps you keep it handy as you practice these four vital strategies for walking in the power of God's Spirit.

KEEP IN STEP

*As you continue walking, you'll find that you are
moving out of your past and into your future.*

CRAIG GROESCHEL

You probably take walking for granted. Barring disease or injury, most people beyond their toddler years don't think about how to walk when they start each day. Walking is one of those basic developmental abilities that allows you to experience mobility. Like those autopilot actions we discussed in previous lessons, walking becomes automatic.

As you probably know, though, being mindful and choosing to walk can be very beneficial to your well-being. There are lifelong benefits of walking as a form of exercise on a regular basis. But many people don't take walking as seriously as they should.

Depending on your level of fitness or athletic inclination, you may overlook or ignore walking as part of your workouts. After all, everybody walks, right? What is so hard about putting one foot in front of the other and taking step after step? Serious runners may be especially skeptical of walking since they're used to taking their ambulatory momentum to the next level. Walking for your mental and physical health might not seem as beneficial as a "real workout."

But many experts disagree. Dr. Matt Tanneberg, a sports chiropractor and certified specialist for strength and conditioning, works with elite athletes but believes the benefits of walking make it ideal for a variety of people at every fitness level. "Walking can be as good as a workout, if not better, than running," he says. "Walking is a lower impact exercise and can be done for longer periods of time."[37]

Whether you're a fitness walker or not, if you've made it this far, you're definitely a spiritual fitness walker. Keeping in step with God's Spirit is the secret to experiencing and sustaining change. You don't have to run, and if you fall, then you get back up.

You just keep walking.

- How often do you walk as a health-and-fitness activity? What do you like about walking compared to other forms of exercise?

- On a daily basis, how mindful are you of walking in the Spirit? What does keeping in step with him look like in your life right now?

- When you stumble because of a bad choice or misstep, how long does it usually take you to get back in step with God? What can you do to get back on your spiritual feet as quickly as possible?

- Based on all you've covered and absorbed in this workbook, what would you say is the key to walking in the Spirit? Why?

EXPLORING GOD'S WORD

Hebrews 11 is often called the "faith hall of fame." It's quite the biblical who's who list, along with each individual's outstanding displays of faith. Before beginning the list, however, the passage begins with the definition of faith itself: "Now faith is confidence in what we hope for and assurance about what we do not see" (verse 1). The "ancients . . . commended" (verse 2) include Abel, Enoch, Noah, Abraham, Isaac, Jacob, Joseph, and Moses, just to name a few.

While this roster is impressive, what is inspiring is that there's clearly room for more honorees—including you. These pioneers of the faith support your journey, cheering you on and reminding you of what they overcame to experience miraculous changes in their lives. There's a sense of them telling you, "If we did it, you can too!"

And you can. Read through the following passage and answer the questions that follow as you consider what dramatic display of faith you might one day be remembered for.

> [1] *Therefore, since we are surrounded by such a great cloud of witnesses, let us throw off everything that hinders and the sin that so easily entangles. And let us run with perseverance the race marked out for us,* [2] *fixing our eyes on Jesus, the pioneer and perfecter of faith. For the joy set before him he endured the cross, scorning its shame, and sat down at the right hand of the throne of God.* [3] *Consider him who endured such opposition from sinners, so that you will not grow weary and lose heart.*
>
> **HEBREWS 12:1–3**

- Read all of Hebrews 11 and notice both the individuals and the reason their faith is honored and remembered. Which individual listed do you identify with most at this stage of your own faith journey?

- As you look ahead at the months and years to come, how would you describe the race that God has placed before you? What do you need to throw off in order to run without entanglement?

● How does the example of Jesus inspire you to keep going when you're weary and losing heart?

● Fill in the blanks: By faith [your name] _____
was known for [the changes you're pursuing] _____
_____.

EMBRACING THE TRUTH

As you try to keep in step with the Spirit, it might feel awkward at times. Similar to a baby learning to balance and take his or her first steps, you may feel a little unsteady occasionally. But that's okay. You're moving forward into new habits and experiencing change in your life like never before. You're learning to rely on God's power instead of your own willpower, and that shift in itself can be new and unfamiliar at first.

During those moments when you may struggle to stay in step, don't forget the adventure you're on. You're on a journey with God that will allow you to experience him in fresh, intimate ways. At times, this new direction may seem scary, but it's also liberating and exhilarating. You're not who you once were because you're changing as you walk with God, moment by moment, day by day.

Along the way, picture God cheering you on as you step out in faith. He is excited for you and delighted by the opportunity to be in a deeper relationship with you than you may have allowed in the past. He wants you to succeed and to enjoy the blessings he has for you in this life.

So don't put off another moment living the life God has for you. Don't find excuses or slump into skepticism based on past attempts. Today is the day. Right now is your moment. Take a step with the Holy Spirit. Then another. And another.

- When have you felt unsteady on your feet while walking in step with God's Spirit?

- What sometimes prevents you from believing God is truly rooting for you to succeed? How do you handle those distractions?

- What are some of the past excuses and delays that have prevented you from starting new habits? Why will they not interfere this time?

- What is one next step the Holy Spirit wants you to take today?

CHANGING THE WAY YOU CHANGE

When students graduate or complete their sequence of courses, the milestone is usually called "commencement." Instead of defining the end of a season or that part of their journey, commencement reminds everyone that they are beginning something new. Just like you.

In fact, consider yourself a student as well as a spiritual walker. Because when you're living in the Spirit, failure is no longer an option. If you slip or stumble, use it as an opportunity to learn what God may want to teach you. Pay attention to where you're going.

Keep walking in the Spirit, not in your own power but in God's power. When you do fall, don't stay down for long. Just get back up. Keep walking in the Spirit.

That is what winning looks like now. There is no such thing as losing. You're in this for the long haul. Remember, it's about progress, not perfection. So when you're winning, you're winning. When you're losing, you're learning.

Either way, you just keep moving forward.

- Look back through the lessons in this workbook. Which stand out to you? Why?

- Do you believe that you can't lose now? What have you already learned from your past mistakes?

- Think about when you first started this workbook to help you go deeper with *The Power to Change*. What do you know now that you didn't know then? What difference does this knowledge make?

- If you've completed this workbook, consider it a huge win! How will you celebrate?

KEEPING THE CHANGE

Think about the ways you wanted to change when you began this workbook. Both the habits and benefits you wanted to add as well as the behaviors and destructive patterns you wanted to eliminate. You're not there yet—but you're on your way!

You catch glimpses up ahead, but you don't want to get distracted or have your attention diverted. Keep your eyes on Jesus. Keep in step with the Spirit, while depending on God, moment by moment. Yes, it will take time, but it will be so worth it. You may miss out on some short-term, fleeting satisfaction, but you know you're choosing the greater reward. You have already chosen what you want most over what you want now.

You can get there. You can enjoy the life you dream about but have not yet experienced.

You are walking, not running.

You can get unstuck.

You, who thought you could never do it before.

You, who are already doing it!

Because you're depending on God's power.

Do what it takes to stay in step with God's Spirit.

You can change!

Your life can be transformed.

You can't. But God can.

LEADER'S GUIDE

This workbook is a companion to *The Power to Change*, and it's designed for both individuals and groups. If you're participating in a group study that has designated you as its leader, thank you for agreeing to serve in this capacity. What you have chosen to do is valuable and will make a great difference in the lives of others.

The Power to Change is a fifteen-lesson study built around individual completion of this workbook and small-group interaction. As the group leader, just think of yourself as the host of a dinner party. Your job is to take care of your guests by managing all the behind-the-scenes details so that when everyone arrives, they can just enjoy time together.

As group leader, your role is not to answer all the questions or reteach the content—the book, this workbook, and the Holy Spirit will do most of that work. Your job is to guide the experience and create an environment where people can process, question, and reflect—not receive more instruction.

Make sure everyone in the group gets a copy of the workbook. This will keep everyone on the same page and help the process run more smoothly. If some members are unable to purchase the workbook, arrange it so people can share the resource with other group members. Giving everyone access to all the material will position this study to be as rewarding an experience as possible. Everyone should feel free to write in their workbooks and bring them to the group every week.

SETTING UP THE GROUP

As the group leader, you'll want to create an environment that encourages sharing and learning. A church sanctuary or formal classroom may not be as ideal as a living room because those locations can feel formal and less intimate. No matter what setting you choose, provide enough comfortable seating for everyone, and, if possible, arrange the seats in a semicircle. This will make group interaction and conversation more efficient and natural.

Also, try to get to the meeting early so you can greet participants as they arrive. Simple refreshments create a welcoming atmosphere and can be a wonderful addition to a group study evening. Try to take food and pet allergies into account to make your guests as comfortable as possible. You may also want to consider offering childcare to those with children who want to attend. Managing these details up front will make the rest of your group experience flow smoothly and provide a welcoming space for group members to engage with the content of *The Power to Change*.

STARTING YOUR GROUP TIME

Once everyone has arrived, it's time to begin the group. Here are some simple tips to make your group time healthy, enjoyable, and effective.

First, consider beginning the meeting with a short prayer, and remind the group members to put their phones on silent. This is a way to make sure you can all be present with one another and with God. Then, give each person one or two minutes to check in before diving into the material. In your first session, participants can introduce themselves and share what they hope to experience in this group study. Beginning with your second session, people may need more time to share their insights from their personal studies and to enjoy getting better acquainted.

As you begin going through the material, invite members to share their experiences and discuss their responses with the group. Usually, you won't answer the discussion questions yourself, but you may need to go first a couple of times and set an example, answering briefly and with a reasonable amount of transparency. You may also want to help participants debrief and process what they're learning as they complete each session individually ahead of each group meeting. Debriefing like this is a bit different from responding to questions about the material because the content comes from their real lives. The basic experiences that you want the group to reflect on are:

- What was the best part about this week's lesson?
- What was the hardest part?

- What did I learn about myself?
- What did I learn about God?

LEADING THE DISCUSSION TIME

Encourage all the group members to participate in the discussion, but make sure they know they don't have to do so. As the discussion progresses, you may want to follow up with comments such as, "Tell me more about that," or "Why did you answer that way?" This will allow the group participants to deepen their reflections and invite meaningful sharing in a nonthreatening way.

While each session in this workbook includes multiple sections, you do not have to go through each section and cover every question or exercise. Feel free to go with the dynamic in the group and skip around if needed to cover all the material more naturally. You can pick and choose questions based on the needs of your group or how the conversation is flowing. Also, don't be afraid of silence. Offering a question and allowing up to thirty seconds of silence is okay. It allows people space to think about how they want to respond and also gives them time to do so.

As group leader, you are the boundary keeper for your group. Do not let anyone (yourself included) dominate the group time. Keep an eye out for group members who might be tempted to "attack" folks they disagree with or try to "fix" those having struggles. These kinds of behaviors can derail a group's momentum, so they need to be steered in a different direction. Model active listening and encourage everyone in your group to do the same. This will make your group time a safe space and create a positive community.

At the end of each group session, encourage the participants to take just a few minutes to review what they've learned and write down one or two key takeaways. This will help them cement the big ideas in their minds as you close the session. Close your time together with prayer as a group.

Remember to have fun. Spending time with others and growing closer to God is a gift to enjoy and embrace. And get ready for God to change your thinking and change your life.

Thank you again for taking the time to lead your group. You are making a difference in the lives of others and having an impact on the kingdom of God.

ENDNOTES

1. "About," James Clear, https://jamesclear.com/about.
2. James Clear, *Atomic Habits* (New York: Avery/Penguin Random House, 2018), 37.
3. Tyler Perry, *Higher Is Waiting* (New York: Random House, 2017), 3.
4. Madeline Berg, "From 'Poor as Hell' to Billionaire: How Tyler Perry Changed Show Business Forever," Forbes, September 1, 2020, https://www.forbes.com/sites/maddieberg/2020/09/01/from-poor-as-hell-to-billionaire-how-tyler-perry-changed-show-business-forever/?sh=6d142f3934b55.
5. "Making History Where History Has Been Made," Tyler Perry, https://tylerperry.com/making-history-where-history-has-been-made.
6. Ruth Perry, "10 Awesome Women Pastors from History," CBE International, March 6, 2018, https://www.cbeinternational.org/resource/article/mutuality-blog-magazine/10-awesome-women-pastors-history.
7. David C. Bartlett and Larry A. McClellan, "The Final Ministry of Amanda Berry Smith," Illinois Periodicals Online, accessed September 8, 2022, https://www.lib.niu.edu/1998/ihwt9820.html.
8. "Michael Phelps," Olympedia, accessed September 9, 2022, https://www.olympedia.org/athletes/93860.
9. Cathy Cassata, "Michael Phelps: 'My Depression and Anxiety is Never Going to Just Disappear,'" Healthline, May 17, 2022, https://www.healthline.com/health-news/michael-phelps-my-depression-and-anxiety-is-never-going-to-just-disappear.
10. Cassata, "Michael Phelps."
11. James Clear, "40 Years of Stanford Research Found That People with This One Quality Are More Likely to Succeed," James Clear, accessed September 10, 2022, https://jamesclear.com/delayed-gratification.
12. Janine Zacharia, "The Bing 'Marshmallow Studies': 50 Years of Continuing Research," Stanford School of Humanities & Sciences, Bing Nursery School, September 24, 2015, https://bingschool.stanford.edu/news/bing-marshmallow-studies-50-years-continuing-research.
13. "Dick Hoyt," CerebralPalsy.org, accessed September 12, 2022, https://www.cerebralpalsy.org/inspiration/athletes/dick-hoyt.
14. Jennifer Ward, "Remembering Dick Hoyt," Ironman, March 21, 2021, https://www.ironman.com/news_article/show/1153584.
15. Ward, "Remembering Dick Hoyt."
16. "Our Story," Guinness World Records, accessed September 11, 2022, https://www.guinnessworldrecords.com/about-us/our-story.
17. "How We form Habits, Change Existing Ones," Science Daily, August 8, 2014, https://www.sciencedaily.com/releases/2014/08/140808111931.htm.
18. "How We form Habits, Change Existing Ones," Science Daily, August 8, 2014, https://www.sciencedaily.com/releases/2014/08/140808111931.htm.
19. Yin, "Secret to Perfect Dog Training."
20. Jeannie Ortega Law, "'The Chosen': Record-Breaking TV Series about Jesus Debuts Worldwide," The Christian Post, December 13, 2019, https://www.christianpost.com/news/the-chosen-record-breaking-tv-series-about-jesus-debuts-worldwide.html.
21. Warren Cole Smith, "A Conversation with Dallas Jenkins – S9.E12," WORLD, November 26, 2021, https://wng.org/podcasts/a-conversation-with-dallas-jenkins-s9-e12-1637860179.
22. "Warren Buffett Biography," Biography.com, updated May 27, 2021, https://www.biography.com/business-figure/warren-buffett.

23. Warren Buffett Biography," Biography.com
24. "What Focus Really Means: Learning from Bill Gates, Warren Buffett and Steve Jobs," Forbes, October 28, 2019, https://www.forbes.com/sites/rainerzitelmann/2019/10/28/what-focus-really-means-learning-from-bill-gates-warren-buffett-and-steve-jobs/?sh=4127487273fc.
25. "Warren Buffet Explains Why He Doesn't Use Twitter and Emails," GuruFocus, April 22, 2017, https://www.gurufocus.com/news/508243/warren-buffett-explains-why-he-doesnt-use-twitter-and-emails.
26. Jonathan Ping, "Warren Buffett Charlie Rose Interview 2022 (Berkshire Annual Meeting)," My Money Blog, April 21, 2022, https://www.mymoneyblog.com/warren-buffett-charlie-rose-interview-2022.html.
27. Alicia Thompson, "Growing Wheat: Bread from the Backyard," Epic Gardening, October 8, 2021, https://www.epicgardening.com/growing-wheat/.
28. Thompson, "Growing Wheat."
29. Ray Bradbury, *The Golden Apples of the Sun* (New York: William Morrow, 1997), 203–215.
30. Faye Flam, "The Physics of Ray Bradbury's 'A Sound of Thunder,' " *The Philadelphia Inquirer*, June 15, 2012, https://inquirer.com/philly/blogs/evolution/Time-and-The-Physics-of-Ray-Bradbury--html.
31. Nick Paumgarten, "Up and Then Down: The Lives of Elevators," *The New Yorker*, July 28, 2014, https://www.newyorker.com/magazine/2008/04/21/up-and-then-down.
32. Paumgarten, "Up and Then Down."
33. Paumgarten, "Up and Then Down."
34. Julie Griffiths, "The Former Drug Addict Who Found God and Built a Successful Business," BBC News, December 12, 2016, https://www.bbc.com/news/business-38220079.
35. Griffiths, "Former Drug Addict."
36. Griffiths, "Former Drug Addict."
37. Brianna Steinhilber, "Why Walking Is the Most Underrated Form of Exercise," NBC News, September 2, 2017, https://www.nbcnews.com/better/health/why-walking-most-underrated-form-exercise-ncna797271.

MORE FROM
CRAIG GROESCHEL

ISBN 9780310151210

ISBN 9780310136828

AVAILABLE WHEREVER BOOKS ARE SOLD.